Film & Tv: A Director's Guide

Kuldeep Sinha

Kuldeep Sinha

ISBN-13:978-1530815067

Dedicated to

all those

Who encouraged and inspired me

to realize my dreams.

TRAILER

Acknowledgment

'I dream films, I talk films,

I think films, I live films

and I sleep with films.'

Raj Kapoor

The great showman of India

Acknowledgement:

The book **'Film & Tv: A Director's Guide'** is the culmination of many years of experience I gained in my association with the marvels in various disciplines of film making those included film directors, editors, writers, sound Designers and many more. It has given me an opportunity to imbibe the intricacies of each department during the production of fiction and non -fiction films. It was my privilege to be associated with them as producer, Director, writer and editor myself for more than three decades.

I will be failing in my duty if I don't mention my alma mater the Film and Television Institute of India which taught me the basics of film making in general and Film Editing in particular.

Shri Hrishikesh Mukherjee, the veteran Film Editor and director in Indian Cinema was always my Inspiration who prompted me to be an Editor first and then be a director. I owe my success and achievements as a film maker to this great film maker of his time. A book on such a complex subject like film Direction cannot be completed without illustrations and references of outstanding film scenes shot by pioneer directors. I bow to all of them who guided many generations of film makers.

Kuldeep Sinha

'Screenplay writing, direction and editing are three basic milestones in the process of a film production.'

Introduction:

Cinema has touched millions of hearts during its more than hundred years of journey. The passion of Lumiere brothers to invent moving images has become a massive craze for the producers and performers, artistes and audience, entrepreneurs and businessmen, young and old alike who made cinema take great strides and attain new heights in entertainment. Cinema has influenced not only our psyche but also our ways of life. This resulted into thousands of young minds dreaming to be a film director whose imagination spilled over the limits of the sky. Though many film schools have mushroomed and books on film direction written throughout the world, there inaccessibility and affordability deprived many such aspiring film makers their due.

''**Film & Tv: A Director's Guide'**, authored by **Kuldeep sinha,** a film graduate from Film and television institute of India and winner of many National and International awards for his films, makes an attempt to fill the void to an extent with its simple narrative and explanation about the fundamentals of film making that a 'Director' must know.

The book "**Film & Tv: A Director's Guide'** in its twelve scenes explains different aspects of film process and technology which includes preproduction preparations, Production planning and precautions, nuances of screen play writing ,shooting on floor and post shooting tasks to be accomplished.

The simple presentation of '**Film & Tv: A Director's Guide'** does not restrict the book only to the students of cinema but those have no knowledge of films may also find it easy to grasp and boost their confidence to realize their dreams to be a film director. The book may open a window to them to peep in to film direction. The film critics and analysts of cinema may also be benefitted by the exposure of practical aspects of cinema explained in the book. The multiple dimensions of the book encourage me to honor Mr. Kuldeep sinha as a **'cinema Guru.'** I am sure this book will be another landmark in cinema writings.

Suresh Sharma

Film Critic (National Award winner)
Dean –Media
Mahatma Gandhi Hindi University
Wardha ,Maharashtra. India

Expressions:

Writing is not only a tool to express myself but also to share my experiences of more than three decades as a Film writer, editor and director with those who can only dream films but cannot afford to make them realize. The success of my earlier books from Cinema trilogy with first one on 'screen play writing' published in Hindi , had a natural consequence for me to attempt a book on 'Film Direction'. While the book on ' 'wr' **Screenplay writing'** introduces the writing ethics and process, the book "**Film & Tv: A Director's Guide'** is poised to guide those who desire to establish themselves as a film director. Another book on cinema trilogy **'The Elements of film Editing'** (English) is available in eBook and Paperback versions in Kindle stores and create space respectively.

Screenplay writing, direction and editing are three basic milestones in the process of a film production. It is imperative for a person to have the knowledge and command over all these three stages if he wants to be a successful Film director, therefore rightly so, these stages are recognized as 'Three steps to be a successful director.' I remember during my days at the film institute of India in Pune, a well known and veteran film director Hrishikesh Mukherjee who was respected more for his Film editing skills, advised the students in one of the informal chats under the wisdom tree that *'If someone has an ambition to be a successful Director he must first learn screenplay writing and the Editing.'* This view of Hrishikesh Mukherjee has long been respected and accepted by many of the top film makers. Due to his proficiency in Film Editing Hrishikesh himself stood tall in the line of successful directors.

It has been my privilege that my book on 'Screen play writing' is not only appreciated by the film makers but also by the experts and the critics in the media institutes. A prestigious SNDT University for women in Mumbai has accorded it the status of an *'Approved reference book'* for its students of Media and Mass communication helping meet the objective for which it is written. The study of all these three books on screen play writing, direction and Editing will be comprehensive and complementary for the intensive and systematic knowledge of film making in its entirety.

Author

Email: kuldeepsinha9@gmail.com

From the heart:

It was my destiny that took me to film institute in Pune. It was only film institute that could open the doors for my entry in to Films. Hailing from a small town of Jhansi in a large north Indian state , I always dreamt to be a film writer and director however I was the lone bird chirping this tune in my family amidst many descending voices from my siblings and parents as well. The film profession was never considered to be worthy of any social respect in those days when parents desired their children to be a doctor, engineer or a teacher or get into a secured government job even if it was to be a low paid clerical one. A secured job was always considered to be the best option and film industry never fitted in this criteria. I was forced to prepare for pre- medical examinations. I felt like running away from home to peruse my creative interests when I came across a notification for admission in various film courses at film institute. It was a blessing in disguise for me and I applied for admission with the lone support of my elder brother Ashok Sinha who was convinced about my passion for cinema.

It was a rigorous national selection process from a written test to an Interview. There was always some divine power to help me clear all the phases in the process and finally I saw my name appeared in the list of the selected students in Film Editing . I had no other choice but it was an irony that I and no one in my family knew what '**Film editing**' was about, at the most they could relate the role of an Editor with a pen in his hand and a paper on his table as in Print media however everyone rejoiced my selection in the film institute. Though I should also have been the happiest man on this achievement, my eye lids did not shut down for long time with a fear of entering in to a field I never thought of. I always wanted to be a writer or a director. It was like falling from fire to the frying pan. I was not prepared to be an Editor but it was only an escape route away from the conservative thinking of my family, if I wanted to make a mark in cinema.

I was groping in the dark with absolutely no idea about the way I was to proceed with the course. I thought, I must be learning the basic elements of film editing in theory and most of the practical sessions would be 'automatic' or 'mechanical' but I was wrong. Film Editing unlike today was completely manual whether to roll or unroll a film, winding and spooling of celluloid film reels, cutting and joining the film frames with the help of scissor and a chemical solution called film cement to firm up the film joints , running and stopping the film rolls speeding on the Moviola, a machine to view the film and stop on a frame for marking etc. The entire process was not only time consuming and tiring but also damaging the palm which used to get cut by sharp edges of film strips and burnt with the chemical reactions while it was applied for joints. I was completely dismayed and disappointed with the process. With each passing day I developed dislikes for the work. I never knew if what I was doing was really editing? I was not the only one to have such a disillusion about film editing but there were few others too. Incidentally few of them had left the course mid way and returned home but I was not that lucky to turn my back as it was me who staked everything including my further studies,   relationship with my family members who opposed my film dreams tooth and nails,, my reputation with my peers who were proud of me when I was selected in a prestigious film school of the country; a privilege to few lucky ones. I had no alternative than to pursue my stint in the film institute however the days were not sunny. I continued to be a reluctant student of cinema till one day there was a surprise visit of **Hrishikesh Mukherjee,** the ace director and a renowned editor in films who was fondly called 'Hrishi da'. I had grown up appreciating his films since my childhood and heard a lot of his editing skills. I decided to meet him but it was not only me, almost everyone was in queue to meet him. They wanted to develop their network for an opening to associate with him once their course was completed, some actors wanted to break the ice for a lead role in his films while few others wanted to begin their career in cinema as his assistants so everybody had a different motive to meet him. I wanted to meet him to ensure if I had taken up the right course. Incidentally I happened to meet him when he was chatting with students after a film show and discussing the film with the students under the wisdom tree. I arrowed my question to him after telling him briefly about my dreams to be a writer and director in cinema.

'If you want to become a good director, be a good Editor first,' was his cryptic reply. After this I had no more query to be answered. His short and crisp one liner was very well edited and précised. He continued to chat with other students. His one liner was enough to inspire me and get engaged diligently in my learning editing. I was spared of many unpleasant and unfortunate situations which would have followed his negative answer that I perceived it was but I trusted him and took his advice positively. My dreams to become a Director were not shattered but crippled however I saw a ray of hope to make it big in Bollywood.

The veracity of Hrishi Da's words was realized by me only when I landed in Bombay after completing my film schooling. I put my first step forward in direction and later on specialized in shorts and documentary films. While writing scripts for film and short stories I realized how   editing helped me in formulating my story line. In fact mental editing started immediately with the concept and spread over to my subject research and subsequently creating visuals on paper. The editing was a tool to firm up the relevant ideas chronologically which was difficult to change later due to the logical positioning of scenes. The structure thus created was as solid as that of bricks and mortar one. 'Editing' imbibed well subconsciously in my mind, in my thought process, in my creativity, in my imagination and ultimately it reflected in my presentations. Without my knowledge, Editing became an automatic creative force of my day to day working. I am now of the firm opinion that Editing is important not only for a theater or a film director but is important for any systematic presentation. Editing is not just a mechanical procedure but an organizer of our thinking process. To organize our thoughts which often go haywire, knowledge of editing is very important. It is more important for a writer and a director who had to pick up the ideas which appeal. The truth of Hrishi da's words was tumbling out one by one . I am sure other successful directors too must have realized it at some point of time during their career.

With my above confession, I appeal to all those who aspire to be a director and those who are reading this book **'Directing films'** should make extra efforts to learn fundamentals of Film editing , I am sure they will be loaded with extra energy and confidence to become a better director than those who don't learn it.

Kuldeep Sinha

'If you want to become a good Director,

Be a good Editor first.'

-Hrishikesh Mukharjee

Ace Indian film Editor & Director

Scene 1.
Film Direction: An Introduction

As a youngster, like everyone I too had a dream to be a film Director. I thought it could remain just a dream as all the dreams don't come true. Children in middle class families normally are pushed to be a Doctor, an Engineer, a bank employee or a government servant. Professions in Films, theatre, music and other performing arts etc. are still not considered respectful in the society therefore many creative dreams are shattered before they could be realized. In the teenage, inherent talent normally raises its creative head very aggressively, people are full of dreams including day dreams and I was no exception. I started expressing through writing lyrics and poems, short stories, drama and novels more often with romantic connotations. I too might have become a doctor like others but for the appreciation I received for my first novel **'Udte Panchi'** (The Birds are flying) from one of the most famous and decorated historical author Dr. Vrindavan Lal Verma who is known for his novels like 'Jhansi ki Rani', 'Mrignayani' and many more gems. His appreciation had not only changed the course of my studies but gave a new dimension to my imagination and creativity. My dreams took a turn and instead of dreaming to be a 'Doctor' I started dreaming to be a *'Film Director'*.

The road ahead was full of pits and falls. Breaking away from the conventional ideology and traditions, dreaming for a disrespectful film profession was as tedious as a disable climbing a cliff. I had no asset except my creativity and imagination along with my strong will power and firm determination. Film institute of India in Pune which was unknown till then, started making news. Film institute could pave the way for me, I thought, but it was almost impossible for me to be at its doors. Swinging in hopes and desperations I bought a lottery ticket probably my first and the last from my meager pocket money which was not enough to meet my daily expenses. I dreamt to be rich overnight and produce my own film in case I won the lottery and become a director myself. One day I dreamt directing a film with the top stars of the time including Jeetendra, Navin Nishchol and Sharmila Tagore in a magnanimous film set. Like every dream this too was destined to be short lived and I fell on the ground of reality but this dream cemented by determination and will power more solidly. I lived films in twenty four hours in my thoughts. The desire to be a director became a burning passion as if my life was a film screen that projected cinema through days and nights.. My vision blurred with cinematic visuals of whatever I saw happening before my eyes. This Passion helped me to travel a long way to realize my dream and the Film Institute playing a stellar role in this journey.

The picks from the pieces of my life have a definite purpose to tell you that the following qualities are a '**must**' for a person who wants to be a film Director-

1. Imagination
2. Creativity

3. Expressions
4. Determination
5. Passion

Imagination:

The unbridled imagination is the take off point for any creative pursuit whether it is film, Theatre , painting or writing etc. The imagination is sometimes influenced by the incidents and happenings around us which affect our life significantly in one way or other. Imagination tries to analyze and understand a specific viewpoint or ideology to form another and different opinion which could be diagonally conflicting with others or contradicting a common notion in variety of ways. This viewpoint or ideology is reflected in creative expressions that separates an artist from another.

Creativity:

Creativity is required to unify various view points, ideology, information and ideas in to one homogenous concept and expression similarly as flowers and leaves of different colors and families are threaded to make a beautiful garland. The creative talent varies from one individual to another due to their differences in upbringing, family values, social and economic conditions and educational merits etc. There can be no standard parameter for creativity in a person however it can be measured only by the success of the outcome.

Expression:

If a painter cannot communicate with his viewers though his colors it is the failure of his expressions. He is failed to chronologies his vague and scattered pieces of imagination in to a meaningful communication. Incomplete, distorted, meaningless and confused expression wastes all the best efforts engaged to accomplish a great 'creation'. Clarity in expressions is as important for a director as it is for anybody else including a dramatist, writer, actor and other creative artistes. Even in our day to day communication we may be utter failure due to lack of clear expression.

Determination:

Determination is the key for the success of a person to meet his objectives. It is important for the success in any profession or business, it is more and definitely if not equally important for a film Director because film making is just not another job but it is the assimilation of many creative streams such as Drama, writing, painting, construction, music or acting and many more. A film director must have the functional knowledge of all the creative and performing arts besides having the knowledge of film technology. Lack of this knowledge will be a definite disaster for everybody involved in the making of a film so there requires a **'firm determination'** to acquire such knowledge and expertise for a person who dreams to be a 'film Director'.

Passion:

In one of the statements the great showman of Indian cinema Raj Kapoor said, *'I dream films, I talk films, I think films, I live films and I sleep with films.'* It's true. No more words are required to define 'passion' for a film maker. Such was the passion of Raj Kapoor that made him one of the highly successful film directors in the world. There cannot be a substitute for an unflagging passion. Nothing should be more important for him than the thoughts of cinema when he is awake or when his eyes are shut.

Process of writing, Production and direction are the basic ingredients of film making. These jobs can be undertaken by a single person or can be delegated to others who have required skills and resources. The jobs can be performed by a 'Team' formed for specific purpose like there can be a team of writers who can subdivide the work of a story writer, a dialogue writer, a screen play writer among themselves however the screen play should always be written by a single writer to maintain the consistency of thoughts, moods and emotions, pace and space, the continuity of characters and events etc..Recently I have come across a review of a much awaited and costly film 'Wazir' which has been rated less than an average film by critics. The top star cast too failed to do justice to their roles due to serious lapses and inconsistencies in the screen play. Here it is amazing to know that the film's screen play has been jointly written by five top writers in the film industry. With such a mix of writers, a hotch-potch script could be anticipated by the producer who himself is one of the top directors with many memorable Films to his credit. Sometimes a producer engages top writers because he may not have enough confidence on his director. In such a scenario while the film may excel in all the technical departments, it fails in effective narration and communication. Sometimes even such teams are subdivided in to 'sub teams' for writing variety of specialized scenes and dialogues etc. it is not uncommon to have number of writers in the writing department of a film production house under the supervision of the director but it is impossible to have a team of directors to make one film however specialized directors can be engaged as and when required to shoot action sequences, song and dance performances or special visual effects etc. These jobs can be clubbed in the following manners-

1. **Director,**
2. **Producer,**
3. **Producer-Director,**
4. **Writer- Director,**
5. **Writer- Producer,**
6. **Writer- Producer- Director.**

In the above clubbing it is clearly established that a single person may be equipped with other experiences and expertise but like a captain of a ship or a conductor of an orchestra ,the film Director must be empowered with all the authority and controls in the entire process of film making. Shooting is another important stage of a film. Just imagine that there are many captains in a ship which is caught in a storm or more than one conductors in an orchestra then what happens if all of them pass different and contradictory instructions to the crew members and would not allow their performance to be fine tuned, it will be a disaster. . Sometimes a director confines himself only to the directorial limits. The Producer takes the responsibility of writing the screen play. Director only shoots the film and is involved only up to the editing of 'Rough cut' of the film. That's why it is called '**Director's cut**'. Thereafter the producer with the help of Editor completes the '**Final cut**' for the release. It may so happen in such cases that the final cut is completely different than the Director's cut. This practice is commonly adopted by the western studios where a producer finalizes a subject and gets the screen play written before a Director is engaged. This has never been practiced in Bollywood however with the entry of corporate houses in the film and television sector sometimes it is possible that production houses may require a Director to translate their pre-written screen play to a film. The entire control from casting to marketing and release of the film is vested with the corporate production houses. The stake of the Director, collaboration and the value of his contribution is another important factor that marks his 'Importance' in the film.

The directorial techniques and process are more or less very similar in various audio- visual productions however they vary in content, recording medium, presentation style, Viewing conditions and the quantum of viewers etc. Such variations can be seen mainly between cinema and television. It is well known that cinema basically started in **'Silent'** form. Later 'sound' was added to visuals but television which came much later than cinema was an offshoot of **'sound Broadcast'** (Radio) where 'visuals' were added .It was actually an Audio-Visual broadcast that was named as 'Television'. In subsequent years cinema and Television influenced each other and narrowed the technical divide between them to outdo the other one. With the growing popularity of Television, big producers in cinema started experimenting with newer and more innovative technologies like Cinemascope, Panavision, 70mm, stereophonic sound to Dolby recording to provide its audience a wider screen experience which was not available on Television. On the other hand improved lighting, set designs, easy camera and editing technology had encouraged low budget art film producers to jump into the television productions. Rising popularity of television in the later years attracted corporate houses to have their own Television channels and production houses competing with their counter parts in film making. Many of the popular and established film studios in the world have not only diversified in to television productions but also established their own television channels to exclusively telecast their films complementing two different mediums of Film and Television.

The technical revolution in television has transformed its form to a great deal. The Television initially took off with direct telecast of live events of sports, political and cultural congregation etc. This fascinated viewers sitting in the luxury of their homes virtually feeling their presence on the actual location to watch the events live. Later Television started beaming recorded programs or previous recordings from the archive after some lapse of time. It is called **'deferred Telecast'**. The documentary, drama or any other show is normally recorded earlier and edited to telecast later. Initially all the television productions were shot on celluloid like cinema, as video/digital technology was not developed to the extent it is today, therefore influence of cinema was very evident in various technical processes. Now with digital technology in vogue the television production from shooting to editing has become much more economical, less time consuming and more quality oriented. While creative functions remained similar to that of cinema, with the push of buttons the operational processes for television have become much easier. For an experienced director production for Television has become a child's play.

Similarly the Television has also influenced cinema technology in a great way. Earlier films were shot by a single camera and director and the cameraman waited for days for the rushes to see before reshooting if required. Today with the use of multi camera set up and Reflex view finder images one can see simultaneously what is being shot or replay the recorded shots later virtually deleting the time taken for the preparation of rushes in the film laboratory. This helps director and the cameraman to reshoot for any lapse during the shooting and the producer saving a significant expenditure and time. Multiple cameras also allow simultaneous editing of the scenes on the vision mixer particularly when it is a live performance. Director has an option to edit the same later if required.

XXXXX

'Film is a director's medium whose work starts with the seed of an idea of making a film. It is the director who first assimilates the story idea in to a screenplay and makes out a systematic plan to translate his imagination to the film.'

Scene 2:
The silent cinema

Film is a transformation of an illusion to the creative realism through moving images recorded on the raw stock of picture negative and sound tapes during the shooting of a film. This transformation takes place by the creation of proper images, proper timing and proper placement of shots in chronological order of the script to provide an illusion of a real action in continuity.

Lumiere Brothers:

The advent of **silent cinema** in the late nineteenth century was in fact the capturing of real activities or events in a single shot by Lumiere brothers without a preconceived idea , a story line or a rehearsal by the performers. The purpose of these films was to entertain the captive audience by projecting the reality on celluloid film through moving pictures. The movies were a step forward of the earlier still photography. These single shot films by the Lumiere brothers included, **'A train leaving the station'**, **'Baby at the lunch table'**, **'A boat leaving the harbor'** and many more. The entire action was generally covered without a cut. Where there were more than one cuts in the action, each shot was cut and pasted together in such a way that entire action looked like a single continuous action but these multiple cuts were absolutely not planned and preconceived. The purpose of the multiple cuts with captions in between was to present the movement in the most realistic manners maintaining the continuity of actions.

After experimenting with the '**presentation of reality**' the Lumiere brothers moved one more step ahead to '**create an action'.** He pre planned the shoot in the film **'Watering the garden'.** A gardener is shown watering the plants in a garden with a rubber pipe. A cute baby enters and puts his foot on the hosepipe stopping the flow of water. The gardener is surprised at the sudden stoppage of the water flow. When he looks at baby, he releases the pipe and water flows out gushingly to wet the gardener. Seeing him wet, the child starts laughing.' This was the first experiment in the history of silent cinema by the Lumiere brothers to make a film with the sole purpose to entertain people with a preconceived story and pre planed action.

Following the footsteps of Lumiere brothers **George Melies** did another experiment by creating special visual effects or trick photography   in the camera itself while shooting a film. Thus the practice of taking a scene in a single shot was at halt.. This enhanced the possibilities of better story telling including special effects to make a film more interesting and entertaining. While the   single shot series of   films   by Lumieres did not exceed the length of more than 50 ft each, the film **'Cinderella'** (1899) made by George Melies was much longer in the length of 410ft.. The 'Cinderella' was shot in 20 parts, each part of the film was similar to the 'one- shot films' of Lumieres however every part of Cinderella' was inter connected with other to take the story forward unlike the films of Lumiere brothers which were complete in a single shot. Revolving around a single character of Cinderella, the film had a definite story line with each part having a different title such as, 'Cinderella in her kitchen', 'The ferry, mice and Leaches',' The triumph of Cinderella' etc. 'Cinderella' was the beginning of fiction films based on a preconceived story with characters and preplanned shooting style engaging actors to play the characters in a film. In subsequent years more experimentation was carried out for a better and effective story telling.

In another landmark experiment Melies used his camera as an audience. The way people sitting in front watch an action played on the stage in a theatrical production, Melies fixed his camera among them to cover an action on a fixed background. In 'Cinderella' and other productions of George Melies, though the continuity of story content was maintained, it was missing in context of the background, actions, continuity from one shot to another and the timing etc. captions were used in between the shots to carry forward the story idea. Influenced by the theatre, these films were close to one **'act'** of a stage play therefore it was clear that Melies' style was highly influenced by the theatre.

Edwin S. Porter, the first cameraman of Edison virtually revolutionized the style, presentation and technique of film making in 1902 by his film' **The life of an American fireman'.** Porter was mesmerized by the actions and dare devilry of 'Fire fighters'. He shot an entire operation undertaken by the fire station. While the coverage was very effective, it lacked elements of interest and entertainment . He needed a story to make the film entertaining therefore he introduced characters of a mother and a child who were trapped in the fire . A rescue operation to save them was shot accordingly.

The operation was divided in number of unrelated shots which individually did not convey anything but when joined together chronologically, they produced a different meaning moving the story of the mother and her child forward who were trapped in fire and recued. 'The life of an American fireman' was a remarkable mix of reality coverage and dramatic enactments which kept its audience spellbound till the trapped family were rescued for their utter relief.

'The life of an American fireman'-

Defying his predecessors of shooting an entire scene in a single shot without a cut, Porter conceived a dramatic sequence having multiple shots as under, covering the scene from different perspectives and backgrounds maintaining the continulty of thoughts, action of fire fighting and rescue operation to give human touch with an emotional appeal by introducing the characters of a mother and a child who were trapped in the fire in a building. This made the film more gripping and interesting.

- **The crew of fire brigade moves in to the place where fire is broke out.**
- **A building is in flames.**
- **In the background, the fire van enters in speed and stops.**
- **Orders are given to fix the engine. Water pipes are taken out of the van.**
- **Stairs are fixed on the windows of the building.**

- Water is gushed with speed through hose pipes on the fire spots. (Dissolve to)
- In the interior of the building a mother with her baby are entrapped in the fire and smoke.
- They run around to save themselves but fail.
- They feel suffocated amidst the fire and smoke.
- The lady shouts from the window to appeal the surging crowd to save them.
- She is again entrapped in the smoke and a burning log falls on the bed in the room.
- A fire man (The Hero) breaks open the door with the help of a spade to enter the room.
- He tears the drapers and opens the windows of the room. He orders his other colleagues to put up a stair on the window.
- Immediately a stair comes up to the window.
- The hero lifts the lady on his shoulder like a gunny bag and climbs down with her on the stair. (The scene is dissolved to).
- Exterior of the building is seen burning.
- Lady in her night suit regains her consciousness and requests the hero to save her child.
- Hero calls his men to follow him and returns back with them to bring the child safely.
- He enters into the room through the window. Tension is built up for some time giving an impression that the hero himself is trapped in the fire and smoke and it was difficult for him to come back alive. After some time he is seen holding the child in his arms.

- **He comes down and hands over the child to his mother ending the breathtaking climax to a happy end.**

The story is conceived very intelligently in three parts to approach the climax. First part is the establishment of a problem that is the eruption of fire in a residential building. The flames increase with the flow of the wind. Another part consists of a mother and a child who is entrapped in the fire and smoke. They struggle to save themselves. Third part is the entry of the Hero who risks his own life and daringly gets in to the fire scene to save the lady and her child thus bringing relief to them and the onlookers. The continuity in the action has been maintained by joining shots in chronological order to give a feeling of a continuous fire fighting and rescue operation. The film ends with the resolution of the problem when the lady and her child are saved.

If we take a close look at the difference in the style of film making of both these pioneer film makers, *George Melies* and *Edwin S. porter*, we can easily point out that if George Melies would have made the film *'The life of an American Fireman'*, he would have separated these parts with a Title caption in between to proceed with the story but Porter has treated every shot as a **'unit'** of a continuous action and joined them to carry forward the story without a jerk or a visual distraction. He had reversed the concept of telling one point at a time in a single shot. This has given greater advantage for creative freedom to a director. The continuity of events or action in the scene presented an illusion of reality to the audience for a better emotional connect and grasp. In *'The life of an American fireman'* porter had beautifully combined the reality and theatrical enactments without disrupting the continuity of a story line and action. This was the beginning of **'Fiction film'** making of today. It is another point that modern film makers concoct the reality in the way they interpret it and want their audience to see it the same way.

Another advantage of assembling number of shots to a definite story line is that director can establish the event by squeezing the duration of the whole action which is also accepted by the viewers. *'In the life of an American fireman'* the entire action of fire fighting and rescue operations was contracted to less than 10 minutes of the real time of many hours however the audience was given the psychological feeling of the event in real time. In this film Porter has proved the following points very effectively-

> **1. No single shot can be complete in action.**
> **2. A shot is only a small 'unit' of the entire scene. The way bricks are properly fixed   together one by one with another to erect a wall, proper placement of shots when joined together create a scene or a film. This is the first principle of editing.**

This basic principle of editing was followed more precisely and systematically by Porter in his next film,' ***The Great train robbery'*** in the year 1903. Known for his innovative approach, the **'one shot transition'** was another innovation carried out by Porter in the film. In 'one shot transition' technique an action was divided into many shots and in editing the action was completed by joining shots in the chronological order in the similar manner as we climb up a ladder step by step. The 'one shot transition' was never used earlier by anybody.

The Great train robbery-

Scene 9- Panoramic view of the valley. A group of robbers is running on the horses.

Scene 10- In the telegraph room, the operator with his hands and legs tied by ropes tries hard to reach to his telegraph table but falls down unconscious. His little daughter brings food for him. She cuts his ropes and throws water on his face to bring him to consciousness. He becomes conscious. Fresh with the memories of the robbery he comes out of the room to give alarm.

Scene 11- People are dancing in a hall. The door opens and the telegraph operator enters in semi conscious state. The dance stops and few people come out with their rifle.

'The great train robbery' was technically one step ahead of *'The life of an American fireman'* due to 'different actions' occurring at the same time in two different locations showed simultaneously. This is called '**Parallel action**'. *'The great train robbery'* was a very simplistic narration with effective use of **continuity of action'** 'and '**parallel action'** to convey a story effectively however his presentation had its own inherent limitations as the events were never preplanned, picked up haphazardly and were shot in theatre style keeping the camera at a fixed distance. This restricted the observation and control of the director over the events and actions. It was on the actors to convey the meaning to the audience through their actions, mannerism and expressions. This technique had direct influence of the theatre in its execution. The shots in the chronological order were juxtaposed in the similar manner as we climb up the ladder step by step.

Almost after twelve years **D.W.Griffith** had liberally used this technique of parallel actions in his films. He not only accepted and executed the techniques developed by Porter but also improved them. His creative experiments became mile stones in the history of cinema. To understand Griffith, let's have a look on the scenes and shot composition from the reel no.6 of his film, *'The Birth of a Nation'*-

Film-The Birth of a Nation: Assassination of Lincoln.

Benjamin Cameron comes out of stoneman House with his friend Essle stoneman. They move to a theatre to see a special performance which was also attended by President Lincoln. The performance in the theatre has started.

Scene 1: Title- Arrival of the President Lincoln (Caption) Location- Auditorium

1. Full Shot. Interior, staircase,

The security guards of President Lincoln climb the stairs of the auditorium one after another   and reach to the president's enclosure. After some time president arrives.

2. Mid shot, Interior, President's box.

President's box is seen from inside. His security men guard the box.

3. Full Shot, President's box, Exterior,

President removes his hat and gives to his assistant.

4. Interior, President's box as in shot 2.

Lincoln enters in to his box.

5. Mid shot, Interior, Theatre,

Essley and Ben are sitting in the theatre. They turn to see the president and get up to clap for him.

6.F.S. Stage in the long shot. President's box is on the right.

The audience stands up and turns to clap and welcome the president.

7.Interior, President's box as in shot 2.

Lincoln and his wife bow to thank people.

8.Long shot of the stage as in shot 6.

9.President's box. As in shot 7.

Mr. and Mrs. Lincoln take their seats after thanking the audience.

10.Full shot. Exterior, President's box,

President's security guards come out of the box and take their place. One of them scratches his knee.

11.Full shot. View of the stage from rear.

The performance on stage continues.

12.President's box, as in shot 9.

Lincoln holds the hands of his wife while seeing the performance.

13.F.S. View from the rear. As in shot 11.

Audience stops clapping.

14.Close shot of the stage.

Actors are performing.

15.F.S.Security guards as in shot 10.

A guard feels uncomfortable.

16.C.S.of the stage as in shot 14.

Performance is continued on the stage.

17.F.S.guards as in shot 15.

The guard in shot 15 shifts his chair behind the door.

18.Interior President's box as in shot 6.

Camera is near the box. The guard returns to his place.

19.Close shot of the box nearer than shot 18.

The guard sits in his place.

Scene 2 ,Act-3. Assassination. Time -10.30. p.m.,

20. F.S of the hall, Stage view from the rear.

Lincolns' box is seen through a mask.

21.M.S. Essley and Ben in the hall.

Essley shows something to Ben towards Lincoln's box.

22. Face of John Booth through the mask.

23.M.S Essley and Ben as in shot 21.

Essley enjoys the performance.

24.M.S. Booth in mask as in shot 22,

Face of John Booth in Mask.

25.C.S. Lincoln's Box.

Lincoln watches the program.

26. M.S. Booth in mask as in shot 22.

Face of john Booth.

27. C.S. Stage.

Actors are performing.

28. C.S. Lincoln's box as in shot 25.

Lincoln smiles while watching the act. Feeling chilled he pulls up his coat and wears it.

29. M.S. Booth as in shot 22.

Booth looks up to get up.

30.C.S. Lincoln's box. Interior,

Lincoln watches the program.

31.F.S. Rear view of the stage as in shot 20.

Full shot. Mask is removed to show full view of the hall.

32.C.S Security guards behind the circular mask as in shot 19.

33.F.S.Booth

Booth exits from the door to come near to Lincoln. He peeps through the hole., takes out his pistol and prepares for the next action.

34.C.S. of the pistol.

35. Shot 33 continues.

Booth comes near the door and opens it with some difficulty and enters in to Lincoln's box.

36.C.S. Lincoln's box as in shot 25.

Booth stands behind Lincoln.

37.Stage as in shot 14.

Actors perform.

38. Lincoln's Box as in shot 36.

Booth fires at Lincoln from the back. Lincoln falls down unconscious. Booth escapes from the side steps and jumps out.

39.L.S. Booth reaches to the stage.

Booth screams on the stage.

The story of *'The Birth of a nation'* revolves around President

Lincoln, carelessness of his Guards and his assassin John Booth. This simple story has been dramatized and presented effectively which not only entertain people but keeps them on their toes waiting for the next course of the thrill. Porter might have finished this film in few shots but Griffith has very intelligently divided the entire story into four parts for which appropriate characters were conceived, prominent of them were the President Lincoln and His wife, President's Guards, assassin John Booth, Essley stoneman and Ben Cameron. The group of performers are created for ambience and some dramatic effects in the auditorium. It seems that the group of performers is distracting the attention from the main event but in reality it is not so as the performance on the stage enhances the excitement and builds up tension that keeps audience glued to their seats so the performance too become a part of the dramatization. This makes the presentation more interesting and entertaining. While doing this Griffith has taken due care of principles of continuity and he has never broken it. He has also used parallel actions to show simultaneous happenings in different locations but at the same time. Parallel actions are imbibed so well that they assimilate with the theme very effectively without diluting the flow of the main story. Griffith has also experimented with the technique of **intercutting** which means dividing a shot in many pieces and using them at different places.

The difference in the working style of both Porter and Griffith is that Porter has divided his action into many shots because it was not possible for him to cover the entire action or incident in one single shot due to its duration and magnanimity but Griffith has deliberately conceived a story and characters in many parts to build up the excitement and dramatized the presentation in which ambience played an important role. The ambience helped the audience to be an integral witness of the story and happenings around. This is a great accomplishment of Griffith which separates him and Porter. However Porter's contribution and innovation to deal with a situation that forced him to divide his action in too many shots cannot be undermined. Porter's technique was adopted and improved upon by Griffith that took him one more step forward to advance his cinematic creativity. With number of shots at his disposal for Editing, Griffith acquired extra liberty to be more innovative and experimental. While accepting Porter's traditions Griffith has added new ones in his urge for extraordinary experimentation in cinematic productions.

In the film 'The Birth of a Nation' the director has worked successfully on many deferent aspects to obtain a cumulative effect. Griffith has divided the whole action into many components to recreate a scene. With this he has been able to touch the depth of story telling or narration which had long lasting emotional effect on audience's mind. The detailed description and interpretation of the scene enhances the realism and brings the audience close to their personal experiences which is difficult to achieve in one single shot. Another advantage of having multiple shots is that the Director is able to conveniently manipulate audience's reaction to the ongoing events by associating characters actions and reactions with the main events of the story. The viewer thus starts associating himself with the characters on the screen and becomes himself a character in the situation. Lets analyze 'the birth of a Nation' to understand this factor appropriately.

'The Birth of a Nation' – an analysis:

Scene: The assassination of Lincoln.

- First fourteen shots in the film show the President arriving to the theatre and his welcome by the people present there. A caption here is an indication of some forthcoming danger.

- Next five shots are similar to porter's single shot action that show various actions of the guard, Like scratching his knee, feeling of boredom etc. in the shot no 15 the Guard is feeling uncomfortable, instead of 'what will he do or not do' scene shifts to the performance on the stage which the Guard wants to watch but cannot due to his posting so he moves to the door of the theatre in shot no17, 18, 19 but returns back to his place. This does not in any way distracts the mood and attention from the main event and continuity is maintained properly. In shot 17 and 18 the guards goes up to the door to see the action on the stage but fails to see it and returns back in shot 18 and 19 . Another caption in this place reflects ignorance of the audience about impending danger.

- In shot nos.20-30 director heightens the suspense by showing mysterious activities of John Booth. An attempt has been made to prolong the suspense by interrupting Booth's mysterious activities with other happenings in the auditorium. Thereafter Booth is projected like an ordinary man so that there is no doubt about him. After some time Booth takes advantage of the Guard who once again leaves his place and Booth plans his further action as shown in shot no.33-36.

- Once again action in shot 36 is interrupted to show the actors' performance in shot no.37 thereafter continuation of shot no 36 is shown in shot no 38. shot no 37 does not show anything new but enhances the dramatic effect of the scene. Suspense and horrification has been prolonged artificially keeping the President unaware of the danger therefore in Griffith's editing Drama is created in extended and simplistic form to avoid uneasiness and artificiality for the viewers.

- In shot no.21 Essley points at the Lincoln. It gives a hint for some time as if Essley has seen the assassin and some mishap is presumed. The audiences thus look at Essley with some hopes that he would take some action to prevent the mishap. In reality this shot of Essley has no meaning in the scene but it helps in increasing the suspense and drama. Before the assassin fires at the Lincoln, though the President is unaware of the future events, it seems that he could do something to avoid the unforeseen occurrence but it does not happen. His actions are considered to be his normal activities before he is murdered.

Griffith had realized that Porter's single shot taking technique in which camera was placed at a fixed distance to shoot like a stage performance, had its own limitations. In this style the viewers could only see the events from the perspective of a fixed distance. Actions performed from other variable distance may not be visible so the actions and reactions of other performers at varied distances were not possible to register in

Porter's technique. To solve this issue Griffith had divided the entire scene into many fragments (*shots*) . While shooting each fragment he decided the actions and reactions of the performers to be covered by placing the camera at variable distances for dramatic and horripilate requirements of the scene. He placed the camera close to actors to cover their minute reactions. Like wise to establish a location and the ambience, he placed the camera at long distance for a wider view. Thus '**Long shots' (L.S.)** and '**Close shots' (C.S.)** were discovered during the shooting. In this technique the freedom and convenience to place the camera anywhere in between was also acquired. The use of Long shots, even the unrelated to the plot, by Griffith helped creating better dramatics improving the technical quality of the scene. Another important innovation by Griffith was the use of **'Flash back'** which became an important vehicle to convey actors' emotional state, memories of the past and events, his ideas and thoughts to the audience. Griffith experimented with this technique freely in his next film *'Intolerance'*. He mixed 'flash back' shots with the present one very simply to relate the present with the past. In such combinations, narrative continuity of the story is more important than the physical continuity.

The greatest advantage of fragmenting a scene into many shots is that the director is not dependent on shooting the entire scene in a single shot nor he has to wait for the entire performance to take place at a time as the actions could be decided as per the requirement irrespective of the magnanimity and the duration of the scenes like war scene ,a gathering a celebration or a protest and procession etc. Everything could be shot in fragments with short enactments/actions as required in the shot however it made a bit difficult for performers to act in close shots; they were so far used to act for an audience sitting at a distance where they could hardly see their minute facial expressions. While Close shots were difficult for the actors, their effect on the audience was immense. In Porter's single shot technique actors had to indulge in overacting or loud acting to make an impact on viewers sitting at a distance. With the innovation of Griffith's techniques while the job of actors became more difficult, the responsibility to create dramatic effects had fallen on the shoulders of the director. *'In the Birth of a Nation'* the suspense regarding Lincoln's assassination became more effective with the repeated use of shot no.37 than with the performance of actors. Therefore it is the director who has to decide how and where a shot has to be used to make the scene more effective and thrilling. The impact of a shot is not dependent on the actors' performance as it is on the talent, merit and creative acumen of the director. Similarly how and where the camera is to be placed, at what angle and composition shot has to be taken and how actors move in their actions are better predefined by the director.

The pertinent question that arises with the use of multiple shots is that how long a shot should remain on screen and who decides it? Normally it is a joint decision of the director and the editor. In this context I would like to add a thumb rule that if the scene has to be fast paced, the length of the shots will be shorter and opposite to this if it is a slow moving scene, the shots will be lengthy. The duration of a visual on the screen is directly proportionate to the length of the shot as the universal speed with which a film stripe runs on the projector is 24 frames/sec. Generally action oriented scenes have faster rate of editing /cutting of the shots **(shorter shots /less duration)** than the dialogue scenes **(lengthy shots/longer duration).** The rhythm of the entire film is determined by the director based on the content and requirements of the scenes as there s no formula for determining the pace of a scene.

Griffith very successfully adopted the style of a story teller while narrating his films. The way a story teller engages dramatic elements to sustain the interest of the audience from beginning to end including mannerism of actors, their actions and reactions, ambience etc and approaches to the climax, Griffith too employed the use of Long shots, Mid shots and close shots to provide variety of visual actions and emotions to the viewers to engage them till the end. That's where Griffith has surpassed Porter and he is called '*The father of Editing*'.

It was not that in other parts of the world there was no experimentation in film production. Russian film maker *Eisenstein* had quoted about Griffith In his article 'Dicans, Griffith and the film today', **'Griffith has used literary style in his editing technique and translated the conventions of storytelling of a novelist in his films. Cross cuttings, close shots, flash backs and dissolves too have parallels in the literature which were discovered by Griffith'.**

Griffith had impressed many Russian film makers of the time but they also pointed out certain flaws in his technique such as his use of Close shots only for 'Parallel actions'. Russians have used various shots to make a '**Montage**' which had a different cumulative meaning and effect than the meaning and effect of individual shots. According to this experiment **'when more than one shots are joined together they have different meaning and effect than that of the original one.'** Its parallel can be found in *'Figure of speech'* in the literature where every word or phrase when combined with others gives a different meaning. A figure of speech is a word or phrase that has a meaning something different than its literal meaning. It can be a **metaphor** or **simile** that is designed to further explain a concept or a different way of pronouncing a word or phrase such as with alliteration to give further meaning or a different sound.

This similarity is evident in the *'Montage'* where unrelated shots mean differently when joined together. There were no 'Montage' in Griffith's technique. His close shots, ambience, traits of actors/characters etc were used as an alternative to the dialogues of the main actors. In chase sequences close shots of chaser and chased were alternately used to speed up the thrill and pace of the scene and not for increasing the importance or visual effects of the scene by *'Juxtapositions'* of the shots differently. Since the films made by Griffith were in their incessant years of development, his limited use of the shots should not be underrated but it should be accepted as another step in the growth of cinematic explanation. Subsequent film makers after Griffith not only used shots as a tool for story narration but also experimented for developing new editing techniques and deriving newer interpretations, intellectual meanings and effects.

According to *Eisenstein*, 'film making in Russia was limited to the advertisement films to promote products and political ideology. Film production was not an organized industry at that time which restricted the knowledge, vision and imagination of film makers in Russia. Griffith's techniques and inventions have provided them an opportunity to think and explore the possibilities of development of films in their country. They picked up the basic theory of film editing from

Griffith and worked to develop newer techniques and principles.' Neo film makers used film as medium to propagate their ideas among them *'Pudovkin'* and *'Kuleshov'* marked their presence in golden letters in the history of cinema.

Pudovkin:

Pudovkin worked to rationalize the basic principles of film making propounded by Griffith. While Griffith believed in resolution of the problems as per his needs, Pudovkin had pre-empted and assessed the issues to develop a new working system which is very important to the contemporary film makers even today. Pudovkin had formulated the guiding principles and systems of editing for the generations of film makers.

To understand Pudovkin's principles of Editing, we have to analyze the role of a director. Apparently a scene shot in fragments (shots) by the director arc not more than unorganized and incomplete pieces of celluloid which have no meaning as they don't convey anything individually. These shots are taken to cover different actions from different viewpoints and perspectives which are not conveyed. It is like an organization of words to make a sentence which has a meaning than that of words used in it as a word individually is useless and non descriptive. Similar words in different sentences convey different meanings. In the same manners each shot is only a fragment of an action and not the whole action. Therefore the exposed raw material brought by the director in fragmented form does not present a complete action, its timing and locations. These shots have to be organized systematically as per the editorial principles and practices to create a meaningful scene which depends on the imagination, merits and creativity of the editor and the director of editing. While giving these shots a 'film form' unwanted actions and reactions, various intervals and gaps are removed. The editor has a liberty to decide about the timing of a shot to remain on the screen as per the requirement of the scene. This is called '**constructive Editing**' as per Pudovkin's principles of editing. The creative or constructive editing can be understood by the following example .Many times we are awed to see a character jumping from the height of a tower or so but the director picturises this action as under...

First of all in shot 1, the actor jumps from the height on a net spread down below. This net is not seen on the screen. In the second shot, the actor jumps from a lesser height to the ground. Both the shots are joined together in such a way that the action from top to the ground is seen continuous one. Therefore it is not really a dangerous action of jumping from a height to the ground as it is made out to be but is an outcome of editorial juxtaposition to create an emotional impact. Special attention is given to maintain the continuity of action by deleting unwanted intervals and gaps, waiting or getting up of the character etc. It is not a photographic trick or special effect but a presentation of an action by using editorial practices.

Pudovkin has converted Griffith's editing practices in to principles of editing. Griffith's use of Close shots to create dramatic effect was completely different than Pudovkin's division of the scene into shots. This 'pre shooting shot division' is now followed by the director during the shoots. Thus the editorial process for a director starts with the beginning of screen play writing itself.

Scene -1:

'A horse cart of a farmer is moving slowly on countryside's muddy pathway of a village. The cart is stuck in the mud. The disgusted farmer pushes his tired horse to move ahead. At a distant corner of the cart a human shape appears out of the dust storm. She wraps her clothes around to protect herself from the wind and dust, the passerby stops near the horse cart and looks at it amazingly.

The farmer turns to asks him, 'Is Nakhabin far away from here?' (caption)

The man guides him pointing to the direction. The cart starts moving again. The man looks at the cart for some time and moves on to his route.'

The screen play is generally written in the above format. Since there were no dialogues in cinema in those days, scenes were separated by inserting captions in between the scenes. Director's comments or views about the scene/theme were also captioned in proper places. In the above example it is observed that actions and reactions are minutely detailed like cart's trap in the mud, disgusted farmer, tired horse, emergence of a human shape at a distant corner, wrapping of her clothes around to protect her from dust and gusty wind, surprise of the passerby etc. These details are similar to that of a literary writer creating a visual presentation in his story or a novel with the sole objective of taking his readers to the illusion of actuality from where they could feel the impact of the scene. The writer and the director of a film too have the same objective when they write a screen play. This is the time when the editing pattern of the film is also outlined. The shot division of the above scene would be somewhat like this-

1. **Long shot**-*A farmer on his sores cart going on a muddy path.*
2. **Close shot**-*The cart wheel sticks in the mud.*
3. **Mid** *shot*-*The cart moves slowly.*
4. **Close shot**-*Farmer is disgusted.*
5. **Mid shot**-*The farmer pushes his tired horse to move faster.*
6. **Long shot**-*The cart in the foreground. A human figure emerges at a distance.*
7. **Mid shot**-*he wraps his clothes around to protect from the gusty winds.*
8. **Long shot**-*A passer by stops near the cart.*
9. **Close shot**- *He looks at the cart with surprise.*
10. **Close shot**-*The farmer turns to him and asks:*
11. *Caption-* **'Is Nakhabin far away from here?'**
12. **Mid shot**- *The man guides him to a direction.*
13. **Long shot**- *The cart starts moving again.*
14. **Close shot**-*The man looks at the cart moving away for a while.*
15. **Long shot**- *He moves forward on his way.*

It is amply clear from the above shot division that minute details and facial expressions must be shown in C.S. or M.S.so that viewers can experience the same emotions which would not be possible if the entire scene is shot in Long shot. Though viewers will be able to see the event in Long shot but the appropriate expressions and their impact on them will be missed out. According to *Pudovkin*, 'every shot in a scene should have different effect and meaning unlike in a monotonous Long shot which is occasionally punctuated with close shots or mid shots to show the details. Such shots neither serve any creative , dramatic purpose or reason nor contribute in creative editing therefore they should be removed.' These inferences of Pudovkin were based on some of his own experiences and some on the experiments of *Kuleshov* in the process of editing which he considered was more important in story telling than the visuals.

Kuleshov:

According to Kuleshov's theory, **'By proper juxtaposition a new meaning or interpretation of shots can be derived which is not conveyed by original shots"**. This can be easily understood by the following example-

Shot No. 1.   **Smiling face of the Hero.**

Shot No.2.   **A revolver.**

Shot No. 3.   **Frightened face of the Hero.**

When we look at the above shots in the same order, we see that the Hero is frightened when he sees the revolver. This explains that the Hero is a weak hearted person and his frightened face reflects his cowardice.

Shot No. 1.   *Frightened face of the Hero.*

Shot No.2.   *A revolver.*

Shot No. 3.   *Smiling face of the Hero.*

In the reverse order when we see his frightened face first and subsequently the revolver and his smiling face in the above order, A frightened Hero looks at the Revolver and smiles giving impression of his daring nature who feels happy and empowered with a revolver. Just by reversing the order of the shot we have been able to change the character and his behavior completely. It conveys another meaning and effect of the scene to the viewers. Otherwise all these three shots individually have no meaning but when they are juxtaposed differently, they convey differently. Thus the director can create the required meaning and effect just by shuffling the order of the shots. This is called **'Creative Editing.'**

In another experiment *Pudovkin* and *Kuleshov* juxtaposed three different close shots with a **neutral shot of the Hero** intercut in between.

First shot-   **C.S.**   **A Bowl of soup is kept on a table.**

Second shot-   **C.S.**   **A lady lay wrapped in a funeral cloth.**

Third shot-   **C.S.**   **A baby is playing with her toys.**

When the audience was shown these three shots inter cut with Hero's neutral shots, their reaction was astounding.

First shot-   *Close shot of Hero*

Second shot-   *A lady laid wrapped in a funeral cloth.*

Third shot-   *Close shot of Hero*

Fourth shot-   *A Bowl of soup is kept on a table.*

Fifth shot-   *Close shot of Hero*

Sixth shot-   *A baby is playing with her toys.*

Seventh shot-   *Close shot of Hero*

When the Hero looks at the lady in funeral cloth, the pathetic reaction of the hero was heart touching. Seeing the lady dead, hero forgot to have the soup kept for him on the table. When he saw the baby playing with her toys, he felt happy. The viewers appreciated Hero's versatile performance in these three combinations without realizing that all these shots of the Hero were neutral and devoid of any expressions but part of the same shot (used four times). An intelligent juxtaposition and intercutting gave different interpretation and emotional context to the shots.

There has to be basic material for any creative work which is arranged systematically, according to *Kuleshov*,' for a Musician or composure **'sound'** is the base material which is composed in particular rhythm and pace. For a Painter' his **'colors'** are the basic material which he arranges on a canvas. Similarly for a film maker the **shots** of the exposed film are the basic materials which are joined creatively to produce an effective and interesting scene.' Kuleshov opined that Film art does not begin with the performance of an actor or with the completion of shooting as it is only a basic procedure to prepare the basic material. The film art begins when a director starts joining the shots and achieves the desired effect after many permutations and combination of shots.

Griffith and Pudovkin - a comparison:

The difference between the editing techniques of Pudovkin and Griffith was in the level of emotional impact of the scene. Griffith used to concentrate more on the behavior, movements and mannerism of actors while Pudovkin worked on the details in the shots to incorporate more variety and dramatic effect. It was predominantly achieved through creative juxtaposition of shots. His technique is still followed by many film makers today. Griffith played more on human conflicts and Pudovkin emphasized more on ambience of the story and the surrounding actions. Pudovkin worked on simple plots based on common events where he devoted more screen time to explain the pros and cons and justify their importance.

Film- Mother   Director: Pudovkin

'Mother' is another example of a good continuity and experiment in juxtaposition of unrelated shots to establish the happiness of a man who is about to be released from the prison. Pudovkin has presented the scene very effectively.

According to his own statement, *'In 'Mother', I have tried to impress my audience with the psychological state of my characters along with some experiments in editing. The son is sitting in jail when he is handed over a piece of paper in which it is written that he will be released from the custody next day. I had a problem to show his facial expressions of happiness when he gets this information. Normally, to show him smiling would have not been effective. Therefore First I had shown his trembling hands followed by a big close up of his lower half of the face to include a corner of his lips with a short smile. I had juxtaposed these shots with few unrelated shots of different ambience like shots of brooks, spring flowers, sunrays falling on water, birds playing in a village pond and a laughing child. In this way by juxtaposing few different shots, I could establish the pleasure on the face of the prisoner'.*

When the scene is analyzed, it is not seen to be effective apparently but the director wanted it this way. Showing just a smiling face of the actor would not have the impact director wanted to create. He took the help of those elements from the nature which expressed happiness therefore the director juxtaposed those pleasure symbols from the nature to create a *'Montage'* where physically every shot seemed directly disconnected but each of them had indirect ideological link which expressed a definite emotion. According to *Pudovkin,' if the details of an event in the scene are fragmented and joined creatively, they produce tremendous effect on the audience.'*

Sergei Eisenstein however had a different view. He believed that,' *linking of various shots depicting details of a scene is very normal. To achieve continuous interest and regular flow in the film, it is necessary to incorporate elements of shocks and surprises at regular intervals. With every cut audience must be provided an opportunity to experience 'conflict' and anticipate further possibilities of 'what next'.*

Every shot of a 'Montage' should indicate forthcoming shocks and surprises. Such juxtapositions in editing help achieve the thrill. Eisenstein imagines **'Intellectual Montage'** when he compares cinema with other art forms. The intellectual Montage can be understood by the following interpretation of shots:

Shot of Dripping water + eyes   . =   Sense of crying.
Shot of an ear + close to door   =   Sense of Hearing.
A Dog + face   =   Sense of Barking.
A face + Child   =   Sense of shrieking.
A face + a Bird   =   Sense of singing.
A knife + a Heart   =   Sense of sorrow.

For Eisenstein such '**Intellectual Montage'** is cinema in which each shot has a different meaning and emotion but their content is always 'Neutral'. When these shots are juxtaposed together in the intellectual context, a series of intellectual interpretations is created. Director should choose his shots conflicting with each other and proceed further discovering inherent meanings and emotions of the shots in the content to provide his audience an opportunity to feel shocks and surprises. These shocks and surprises can be created by the variety and contrast in the composition of shots, Distance from the camera, Back ground, Depth of field, cinematographic technology and gimmicks, special lighting arrangements etc. This can also be created by connecting some disconnected shots .The duration of the shock is not important , which can be short or longer as decided by the director.

In the '*Intellectual Montage'* of Eisenstein the problem is not that of the juxtaposition of shots but of how easily the viewers will be able to grasp its inherent meaning and emotions. It is possible that they may not understand it when they watch it first time or they may have to tax their mind to understand by watching it many times for which they may not have the time and patience. In such a situation director may not be able to properly convey what he wants to say. But whatever it may be, by his concept of 'Intellectual Montage' Eisenstein had definitely created a new 'Genre' of film making which can be called' *Intellectual or Experimental Cinema'.*

It is correct to say that only one person is responsible for creative expressions or creative ideas like a painter for his painting, a writer for his story, novel or poetry, a musician for his compositions but it is not so in cinema . In the early phase when films were silent and more experimental, films of Lumiere Brothers might have lacked creativity in expressions as films presented   live events that had no preconceived ideas and exceptional planning. The moving images of 'Arrival of a Train', 'workers leaving the factory', 'A demolition', etc on screen attracted people from all walks of life to a new medium and experience. There were no writers, Recordist or an editor for such films. The director many times himself wielded the camera in the absence of a cameraman. In fact these films were made solely by one man's imagination and efforts. In the year 1903 Edwin S Porter made 'The great train Robbery' with a preconceived action sequence and laid the ground for films on preconceived story line with a well thought of execution plan. He divided the scene in many fragments (shots) for shooting and subsequently joining them in chronological order introducing a new element in cinema called *'Film Editing.'* Porter analyzed the *'space'* and *'depth'* in the moving images to establish a relationship with other images/shots. This resulted in **'visual continuity'** when shots were joined together in chronological order keeping the consistency of Time, Place and the desired emotional effect . Porter is credited for introducing an effective **'Narrative form'** of a storyline which is still accepted by film makers the world over.

XXXXX

Scene 3:
The Director:

The flood of opinions, reviews, acclaims and criticism, data on box office collections and analysis preceding and proceeding the release of a film every week in the news columns of popular and unknown publications and periodicals, cable and television networks, Promotional appearances of stars on television channels present a very subjective and hazy picture of the films' success. Some films are taken head on by the viewers while others are forgotten like a bad dream without a trace in the memory. Some successful films are credited to its excellent direction or writing and few of them ring the bells in the box office revenue for their stars value. It is a fact that a film good or bad is a result of the team work then why only apparently directors or actors are given more credit than other crew members. Everyone involved in the film production from the writer, director, cameraman, recordist, Editor, actors, set designers, music directors, singers etc give their best creative and knowledge contribution to the success of the film. No one actually works to make a bad film then why only actors or directors walk away with all the applause? It is a pertinent question that is not easy to answer due to its complex economics. It is said that *'If a Film is well made and successful it is everyone's credit but if it is bad, lacks standard and quality, unsuccessful to attract people to the ticket counters then it is the Director's failure.'* This premise is purely based on the capacity of the director and more importantly of the actors to draw the audience to watch their films but still director is considered to be more responsible for a well made film than his other associates because a Director is *'the captain of the ship'* who decides the direction ship has to move by giving right instructions to the crew members and the technicians . A wrong move is a definite disaster not only for the ship but also for the entire crew and co travelers. The crew follows captain's instructions to the best of their knowledge and capability. Similarly a film crew follows the director's orders and advice.

Fundamentally **'Film is a director's medium whose work starts with the seed of an idea of making a film. It is the director who first assimilates the story idea and makes out a systematic plan to translate this imaginative ideas to the screen play according to his own vision and perception, likes and dislikes, ideology and interests. Thereafter he has to cross through all the milestones in the journey of film making.** The Influence of a Director's imagination is visible in all his technical moves and decisions including the cast, right from cinematography to the end product. People who are not well versed with cinema may not be aware of the fact that nothing on the screen occurs without the consent and approval of the director.. It is his responsibility and his sacrosanct duty like the conductor of an orchestra to coordinate with all the departments to achieve the best results without leaving anything to chance. If he has to fly birds in a scene, he has to plan for it and execute it at the proper level. It may be noted that everything happening on the screen is made to happen as required in the scene whether it is birds chirping, rains and snow, passing of a train etc. Sometimes a director works out a special color scheme, lighting arrangements, set designing, acting and the dialogue delivery of characters to have desired impact. All the departments extend their full support to him to achieve this objective . The director must have sufficient technical knowledge including knowledge of the society, culture and the traditions of the place, religion, behavior of the people and social groups, life style etc. to guide his crew members and characters during the production process. While executing it he should not ignore the sentiments and values of local social groups who may be hurt by certain projections of facts and ideology to avoid any controversy later.

The differences between a director and his crew members emanate basically from the fact that the director sees the film in totality while others may be restricted to their immediate task. Their knowledge and expertise is limited to their specific job requirements. It is difficult for them to see beyond this point nor it is required therefore the credit for the failure of the film rests with the director. It also implies that the director has failed to take out the best from his crew. Even the best support from his crew may not result in a successful film due to the failure of the director however in a well made film the contribution of all others cannot be undermined. In this background the role of a director gains more importance.

Technically the director is not accountable for distribution, exhibition and the business of a film however while planning a film it is his sacrosanct duty and responsibility to ensure that the film he would make has the potential for doing good business. If it does not make big profit the film should at least recover the investments. Since making a film is a costly proposition therefore the director cannot ignore its economical aspects. It is very common that when director doesn't consider the economics of the film, many of the producers are either doomed and don't return back to make another film. If they don't have any alternative business they sell off whatever they have to make another film .It is generally not a good idea as he may not get any further professional support including finances from other sources and may end up losing everything further. Therefore a director cannot shirk away his responsibilities from the tasks he is directly or indirectly not concerned.

Director's area of responsibilities include: *1.writing , 2.Cinematography, 3.Art direction and set design, 4.Acting , 5.Lyrics and Music, 6.Editing, 7.Sound design and sound recording, mixing etc., 8.Costumes, 9.Distribution, 10.Exhibition, 11. Business and budget, 12.Any other task in the production.*

It is the director who takes the viewers to a journey through his characters that culminates in the climax of the story. In this process Director and his team display their creative and technical excellence that makes this journey interesting and enjoyable for the audience. Director's main job is to create a fine balance between his team members and extract the best out of them. A technically weak director always works under pressure and obligation of his team members which is neither proper nor conducive to his dignity. He is never respected for his lack of knowledge. It also hampers film's quality as everyone in the crew works to his own ego and ideas. They fail to see and understand the film in totality therefore a director must accomplish results to the best of his creative and technical satisfaction.

A film director should keep aside his ego and get completely drenched in the film. His actions, thoughts, imagination and everything else must be centered on making an interesting and successful film although there is no formula for a commercial success.. If there would have been any formula available some where everyone would make a successful and profitable film and no film would have been dumped by the audience. Therefore the director while making the film should not worry about financial success but concentrate on making a technically and aesthetically sound film that appeals everyone.. This works in his favor even if the film is commercially not as successful as expected because everyone from the producers, financiers, distributors or the audience are aware of his sincerity and no one questions his creativity. The film *'Mera Naam Joker'* made by great showman *Raj Kapoor* is a classic example of this contradiction. The film flopped miserably at the box office but later it became a cult film in the history of Indian Cinema. There are many such examples in the film business.

A director always stands on a cross road. On one hand he is responsible to his producer and the financiers, on the other he is also answerable to his audience who expect a certain kind of quality entertainment from him. He is duty bound to fulfill their aspirations. It is this bond with the audience that keeps the writer, Producer and the director glued together to achieve a common cause. Their entire energy, imagination and resources are utilized to accomplish this objective. The three work in complete tandem and accommodate each other to incorporate their audience' expectations from them. The writer and the director together make many changes and continue to modify the screen play to provide their best to their viewers. In the Process sometimes there arise few conflicting situations between a writer and the director which should be amicably resolved by the director without hurting writer's sentiments towards his story. A successful Director always works towards achieving the best results and not for his own glory because a well made film automatically pushes him to his glorious heights. However all this is not a cake walk for him. Besides having technical competence and expertise, responsibility and sincerity he has to display his complete control and authority, unbridled imagination, management skills, patience and sensitivity. He has to lead his team and not be lead by them to avoid a tag of being a mere puppet in the hands of his crew members.

Directorial style:

Every artist or a creative person has his own style of expression whether its writing poetry, story, drama, novel , painting or making a film It is the director's prerogative to define his own style which gives him his unique identity among other directors, The critics review a director's work based on his directorial style and declare merits or demerits of his presentation in proper and clear communication. Every film maker must understand that a film is not made and meant only for the film maker but for the audience who pays for watching a film so there hard earned money should not be allowed to go down the drains. It will not benefit anyone either who has worked for the film or has financial stakes.

In the process of defining his style a director visualizes his locations, special setting and lighting, editing pattern, special performances by actors which reflects director's innermost sentiments and emotions, his creativity and sensitivity. Many directors work out their style in consultation with their cameramen who help them to realize his style the way he has imagined. Once a cameraman starts understanding a director's vision and imagination he gives him advice on specific color scheme, special lighting and camera movements, setting etc. This understanding between them becomes an instrument to create some special effects in the film that matches with his director's style.

Selection of indoor or outdoor locations too reflects director's style. Some director's prefer indoor shoots in controlled conditions of a studio or specially designed sets. It eliminates number of unwanted problems like crowd control, interference of local goons, load shedding , weather conditions and many more. In indoor shoots or in an outdoor set the director has the freedom of fixing camera at his convenient place and angles along with the flexibility in actors' movements, setting, lighting etc. Those who prefer 'reality' in the film opt for outdoor locations however some time for many reasons the outdoor shooting is not convenient as its indoor counterpart. In the outdoor shoot realistic ambience is created. Before embarking to an outdoor location the director must find out weather conditions, power supply, transport and accommodation arrangements, catering and other necessary requirements. If the entire film is planned to be shot on outdoor location the best location must be selected as required in the script. No compromise should be made on this aspect.

There is always a possibility that a location has to be recreated in the studio due to various reasons ,a historical set is to be designed and erected in a studio or outside. In such a situation the art director and the director are required to do a thorough research and work out the minutest details to make it look more authentic, believable, and realistic.

The role of an Art director is crucial in this pursuit who translates his director's vision and creates life in the set however the director should also not leave everything to the Art director but should work out the maximum details as he has visualized while writing the screen play. This conveys a fairly clear idea of his concept to the Art director. Ultimately it is the director who has to approve the sets. if he himself is not sure of what he wants, it makes the job of an Art director much more difficult and complicated and director's approval more confusing. This confusion may also result in wastage of lot of time, money and efforts.

The Audience:

No film can be termed a success without the patronage of its audience howsoever well made it is. Empty ticket counters in cinema halls break the back bone of the Producer. Once the film is bombed at the box office, it is many times an end of the road for its promising producers, directors and the actors. Though the director is equally responsible to his producers and the audience, it is normally not easy to gauge the mood and the taste of the audience for a particular type of movie which can differ from their age group, their literacy level, their social, economic and cultural upbringing and last but not the least, their intellectual quotient. Most of the time a film gets its success though its front benchers and whistling audience who generally come from the lower strata of the society therefore it is imperative for a director to touch the sensitivities of such category. There are normally three types of cine goers. The audiences from all these categories watch a film from different perspective and the purpose.

1. **Low IQ level-** They are people who throng to a cinema hall with a sole purpose of **'money back entertainment'**. They are the most dedicated and regular patrons for a commercial or an entertainment film. They don't shy away whistling in the theater when they watch an action or a sex scene between a Hero and the Heroin or a villain rape the sexy siren or the Hero overpowering the villain etc. These people form the largest chunk of the viewers.

2.**Medium IQ level-** They generally consist of *'Family audience'* who like to see the film with the entire family and prefer to have a **'clean entertainment'** with content, values and traditions like the middle class society which is normally considered to be the gatekeepers of the social and cultural values of a society and the nation. This middle level of the audience preserves the values in cinematic entertainment. Here it may not mean that the people in this category don't come from high intellectual quotients but their preferences are limited to family entertainment.

3. **High IQ level-** People in this category mostly belong to their very rigid political and social ideology who are **opinion makers** and have their own identity. They are the leaders in various fields and professions including cinema. They don't compromise with their ideology for the sake of earning mega bucks from their films. Art cinema , Parallel or purposeful cinema is propagated by these people for these people. These

films are made with a definite purpose to stir the conscience of the people.

The broad categorization of the audience helps a film maker to zero in on the content he would like to produce for the type of audience and intellectual level. When the single screen cinema halls were in vogue the film makers were forced to keep all the above categories of people in mind before embarking on a particular story as films were seen by one and all under the same roof as it was the only and most economical entertainment in towns, villages and the countryside. Though a commercial film is mostly patronized by people of lower denomination a director can simply not ignore other categories of people who walk down to a cinema hall just for entertainment therefore a director has to work out a fine mix of sensitivities in the content for everyone. This need has brought to the fore a new' *Middle of the road'* approach by film makers who pick a sensible and purposeful content and incorporate some ingredients to lure others. While this categorization was blurred during the phase of single screen entertainment, advent of Multiplexes has to an extent defined and segregated the type of people who go to a multiplex with a fixed frame of mind to watch a film that suits to their sensitivities and tastes. It has made the decision making for a director to choose content much easier. This permits a director to chose a target group of his film and decide about the subject. It also facilitates a director to work on the budget of the film accordingly. While the director may choose a particular target audience for his film still he should try to attract as many people as he can within the limitations of his content, budget and quality. Since there cannot be a fixed parameter to assess the intellectual quotient of the film

Film & Tv A Director's Guide

audience therefore without pressurizing and challenging their mind the director should work on a film that is acceptable to maximum people.

Besides being different in their intellectual levels people also differ in their taste, religion, culture and traditions, ideology and perception etc which prompts them to react and behave differently while seeing a film in the captive atmosphere of a cinema hall. It is a great challenge for a director to take forward the sensibilities of everybody through his imaginative and creative story telling from the beginning to the end. In this sense a director can be paralleled with a magician who keeps his audience hypnotized under the spell of his influence and swings them to his intellectual level as and when required. People see and understand what is shown and made to understand by the magician. In the process the magician creates thrills and suspense, shock and awe before coming to a conclusion and release of built up tension.. This continues till the end of the show and the audience is hooked till the resolution of the act. Similarly the director must innovate his story telling in such a way from a problem to the built up of the tension and ultimate resolution of the issue which no one should have anticipated and the audience don't have time to ponder and apply their mind that takes them away from the situation.

The director should be aware about the fact that psychologically a person can react only to one thing at a time. If he has to deal with many problems, stresses and the solutions in the story on screen simultaneously, he will not be able to digest and accept it and will miss out many emotions during the course when he returns to his normal self therefore only one issue must be taken up at a time and resolved before another one is pushed in. It is in the same manners that we can hear only one person amidst many talking together. Even the one who is heard is not clearly understood. This theory applies to everybody sitting in the cinema hall. Every person has some limitations in their seeing and hearing abilities as an eye can see many objects to a long distance but the ear can hear only the nearest one. To counter this issue the director during the recording may give importance and emphasize the sounds emanating from the nearer objects to balance the images and the sounds. The sound distances can be managed by increasing (for nearer objects) and reducing the volume (for the distances) during the recording to give impact of physical distance between the audience and the screen objects.

Recently a typical audience behavior to see a film or not, is influenced by the hype created by the 'Promotional appearances' of the stars on various popular Television channels, film reviews on the release day and almost immediate telecast of the new films after the release has gained importance. The trend is commonly observed with those films which don't do well at the box office. Therefore those who are not keen on seeing the films immediately on the big screen if there feed back or reviews are not inspiring, wait for the films on television to watch them almost free of cost at the luxury of their homes at their convenience. The film reviews are another important factor that influences audience's behavior and decision to walk to the nearest cinema hall.

The competition to grab maximum numbers of screens in the Multiplexes too has reduced the chances to the success of a film. Normally films with big stars with their corporate counterparts vie for maximum screens, sometimes this number is in many thousands for a nationwide release excluding overseas one. This is done to have maximum footfalls to the theater during the first weekend which decides the future collection of the film as it starts receding thereafter in subsequent days and weeks. The fate of other low budget films with not top of the line star cast is sealed due to lack of promotion and less number of screens however it is believed that if a film makes it to the projection machines, normally very rarely it loses money it has spent .The economics of the film does not fully depends on the collection from the theater with many more revenue channels available worldwide. So the concern is not with a film being a flop but how much money it can generate for its producers.

The occupancy percentage in the cinema halls as a parameter for the success of the film is a thing of the past when less than 80% occupancy sounded a danger alarm . Number of weeks a film could run was another criteria for the success thereby concept of *silver, Golden and platinum jubilees* was very popular and the stars in these films were labeled as *'Jubilee stars'*.

The run of the films is not that much a matter of concern for a director as it is for the Producer who is worried for money flowing in to his bank accounts therefore the promotion and the release strategy has become an important factor. The director and the producer together must work prior to the launch of the film, to strategize the business and release plans. While the occupancy parameters are still relevant to the existing single screens, the multiplexes which are generally owned by corporate sector have concentrated more on the total collection as the tickets sold on the counters are not the only revenue source for their survival. The quantum of total collection for a film has given way to the new parameters for the success of the film when they enter in to the Clubs of 100cr ,200cr, 300cr or more depending on their gross revenue collections.

Unfortunately, this rat race for getting in to these elite clubs of successful films has its own pitfalls when economics is given precedence over the aesthetics of the film. The collection is maneuvered by apt strategy for promotion and hype created for a film. This many time results in higher revenue collections by a below average film due to its sheer manipulations of business tactics and fudging the figures.

Planning a film:

It is generally believed that Film technology is merely a tool in creative expressions .A film as a medium is a conglomeration of various art forms that play a very important role in the overall presentation of the film. The film making employs and engages creative people from different walks of art life but the knowledge of film technology is as much important for a film maker as knowledge of a language for a literary writer, knowledge of musical notes and rhythm for a musician etc. The knowledge of technology for making a film is essential but excessive use of technology is an impediment to the effective and expressive communication therefore many film makers don't prefer to be labeled as a 'Technician'. For a cameraman, Recordist, art director , set designer, costumes designer and others 'technology' is just a tool for creative and effective expressions in the entire process of film production. They all work to achieve a common goal to make every scene of the story as effective as they can by using their technical expertise however it is never used to display their 'knowledge'. Their contribution must be a part of the scene and not a show of his expertise as oil on the surface of water.

Many of the film directors these days step in to film making after their stint in Theatre and Television. These directors are normally influenced by their own previous experiences, technical limitations and styles. They lack cinematic expression due to lack of knowledge in cinema technology. While they get the technical support from their crew members, sometime they fail to assimilate and incorporate their creativity and imagination in to their cinematic vision. Therefore it is very important for a director to know the nuances of cinema including screen play writing, cinematography and editing and sound recording techniques to enable him to imbibe them appropriately in his style either for a film or a television show.. The technical knowledge helps a director to have complete authority on his actions and decisions which saves him from inferiority complexes with his unit members.

Budget & Finance:

Preparation of a budget is the first and foremost task before embarking to produce a film. If the director and the producers have not zeroed in to a story ,they can work out a technical budget for the film depending on the broad idea and the type of film director wants to undertake. The technical budget generally excludes variables like actors' remuneration, sets or specific location but makes a provision of average expenditure for them. Though this budget has to be revised later once story and the screenplay is finalized, it helps a producer to know the minimum finance he will require to make a film or a television programe/episode.

Budgeting is the job which cannot be done in isolation either by a director or a producer as it starts from the time a decision to make the film is taken followed by acquiring the story rights, writing of screen play, signing a director, lyric writer, music director, actors and associate technicians, pre and post shooting expenditures including hiring of locations, equipments, Promotion and publicity and ultimate release of the film. The estimation of all these expenditures cannot be made by a producer or the director alone. It requires the services of experienced Production Manager and accountants.

Preparation of budget is an extensive and serious exercise which requires detailed knowledge of every department that needs some expenditure to be incurred during the course of production. Anything left out during the budget making may create difficult situations and expose the producers in bad light. It can have variations depending the genre and magnitude of the film. A budget document may be divided in three parts mainly -

1. **Preproduction-** This includes the expenditure that are incurred from the day a decision to produce a film is taken by a producer. The first and foremost requirement is to acquire a story and decide about the director if producer himself is not ready to wield the megaphone. Thereafter he has to finalize his script writers, actors and other important crew members, art director and set designing. Location survey etc. some producer also prefer to record few songs before shooting to attract distributors and the financiers besides setting up a production office with minimum support .

2. **Production-** This entails major part of the budget expenditures. It includes shooting, hiring of lights and other equipments, set construction, costumes, location arrangements, boarding and lodging of the crew members, Travel and transportation and other shooting expenses.

3. **Post production-** It includes editing, recording effects and dubbing, Rerecording, prints and previews, Promotion and publicity etc.

Following is a broad format to prepare a budget document:

1. **Preproduction:**
   Story, copy rights.
   Producer/Production partners.
   Director.
   Writers
   Main actors
   Cameraman
   Recordist
   Art director
   Editor
   Travel and living
   Song writers
   Music director
   Singers
   Song Recording studio
   Office expenditures
   Assistants' fee
   Publicity Manager
   Production Manager
   Fringes

2. Production:

Supporting and junior artistes

Extra artistes

Production staff

Set construction

Studio/Location charges

Camera equipments

Sound recording equipments

Miniatures

Set operators

Electrical requirements

Special shooting units

Properties and set furnishing

Costumes

Makeup and hair stylist

Choreographer

Action director

Facilities fee

Assistants' fee

Travel and Transportation

Production dailies-food, Daily allowances, conveyance etc.

Accommodation

Fringes

3. Post production:

Editing

Music

Post production sound

Stock shots

Titles

Special effects

Laboratory

Post production charges internal
Promotion and publicity
Fringes

It may be understood that film making does not end with completion of the shooting as is widely believed by newcomers in the profession. They tend to ignore many essential post shooting expenditures to be incurred on preparation of rush prints, laboratory expenditures, editing ,dubbing, special effects, back ground music, Re-recording and the final print etc. Expenses on these accounts are by no means insignificant and cannot be brushed aside just to lure a producer with a reduced budget.. Many of them feel that post shooting expenditures can be met by raising advance money after showing the rough cut to the distributors or by selling rights. It is a tricky situation and could be disastrous as it is decided on presumption and probabilities of a good film being made. The producer who has no experience in the field is easily tempted by the glamour exposed to him by unscrupulous elements who talk impressively to hook a lamb. He commits everything what he has and floats in the air till he finds himself in the hot water but by this time it is too late. It happens mostly in cases with low budget films with comparatively fresh actors and technicians where a producer arranges his finance on piece meal to complete the shooting. It is fits and start for the producer. No one knows in such a situation if a film will at all be completed that too in scheduled time.

With rising cost and competition most of the distributors are reluctant to pay advance to an incomplete film. They buy a film only on its completion with the prospects of their recovery. Low budget films produced by corporate houses are given no different treatment by any buyer of distribution rights unless the corporate house is releasing the film itself.. An analysis in the trade reveals that there are many low budget or high budget films including big stars which are not considered by any distributor even after they are completed in all respect due to their loss making possibilities therefore such film never see the arc light in the theatres. This unfortunate situation can be avoided with proper estimation of expenditures at various phases of production and the assessment of the producer's capability to raise finance in toto. This assessment can be made in two categories: 1. *Finance available* and 2. *Finance committed.* There should never be forced reduction of the budget on any of the expenditure heads. Giving false estimates is an invitation to more troubled times ahead.

Those with limited funds available with them should be more précised in planning every detail of the budget from the beginning to end and be careful in spending during the course of the production. They should be more confident about the story and the contents during the writing of the screen play. Obviously a producer of a low budget film cannot afford the luxury of shooting in many locations and abroad or cannot have a song and dance performance with hundreds of performers shaking their legs. Similarly one should avoid erecting costly sets and shooting action sequences.

Initially one should be prepared to use his own resources or obtain support from his friends and the relatives to start a project due to negative flow of funds . The personal money or the support from others at this stage should always be taken with proper compensation package at a later stage. This should be included in the budget to create trust factor to avoid them thinking that their money would go down the drains. An act of thanklessness towards them is neither congenial nor beneficial in future. Particularly with close friends and relatives as a person in the field of film/Tv production always needs support from people in various forms whether it is personal, financial, loans and borrowings or any other form therefore a Producer should be generous in compensating them for any support rendered to him by others including his crew members.

The director who is in big leagues of the production houses is expected to be creative while also being commercial. A big budget film producer would not take such a big risk without being sure of returns with maximum profits as he intends to continue and make films one after another and not flee away after losing his investments if his film is bombed. He does not make a film for charity; in fact no one does it, not even a small budget producer. Therefore the director cannot lose his sight from the business of the film. He has to be actively participating when the business plan and the budget making is underway balancing his creativity and economics.

A successful director has to fulfill the aspirations of his producers as well as his audience. If a director decides to make a film for his creative satisfaction then he has not only to meet the budget requirements from his own resources but also be responsible for its production as well as its release. He is accountable for all his actions, decisions and deeds without putting blame on anybody else for the consequences. It can be an adventure or a misadventure for him. Therefore it as important for a director to be creative as he is to be a businessman to manage his finances. If a director is able to make a technically sound film keeping the interest of his audience as well in mind, it may not be a daunting task to arrange money though it may take some more time but for this purpose the director must have proven record of his success.

The detailed planning and execution of the agreed plan is one of the toughest challenges a director has to face from the moment he steps out of his comfort zone to his producer's or financier's door. Convincing them to shell out money for his project is like extracting water in the desert because they only see a business opportunity in the proposal while the director is craving for his creative expressions. This task is as daunting for a young director as it is for an experienced one. The difference is of some degrees. Most of the precious time and efforts of the director is wasted in such unproductive activities therefore it is advised that finding a producer and the financer may be completed before a final script is written however many people believe that a well conceived and written script makes the director's job much easier to find sponsors for his film. It may be true in few cases but it is neither a practice nor a guarantee that after a detailed script one gets a producer on a platter as both the director and Producers/financiers work on different planes of *'creativity'* and the *'economics'*.

The tug of war between creativity and the economics is not new in film industry the world over but people are helpless as they cannot bridge the gap. Making a balance between creativity and the business of films is a challenge for a film maker that steals his night sleep and pleasant dreams which he has been weaving for long. Some established the studio system to overcome this problem. In India there were many popular studios Like Prabhat studio, Filmistan, Bombay Talkie, RK Studios, Kardar studio, Mehboob Studio, Kamalistan, and many more spread in other parts of the country which have given a series of classics to Indian cinema. Similarly in USA MGM,, Warner Brothers, Columbia and others have been very popular for more than half century and still going strong. In later years many of the studios have downed their shutters because of rising maintenance cost and land value that tempted them to sell of their properties for commercial constructions at an exorbitant price. These studios engaged creative people on monthly remuneration and the director was given complete creative freedom. Studios took over the business control without encroaching on other's territory. When studios started to shut down, the situation returned to squire one and film and television production once again became more commercial and an unorganized activity. In the United stated studios like MGM, Universal, Warner brothers and many more are still active besides contributing in the technology developments.

Special curriculum in film studies provided by many film schools and the universities all over the world is also churning out meritorious and talented young boys and girls who unlike earlier, made film making their well thought off and considered profession. These youngsters are bubbling with creativity and a business acumen but unfortunately ever decreasing number of films made and rising production cost to stupendous levels is a dampener in their aspirations. Very few of them are able to make their indelible mark under trying circumstances and struggle. Rests are lost in oblivion. The emergence of Television gave rise to new hopes to these young men who saw ample opportunities in Television which has narrowed the gap with films in production and technology but there too things are not very different than film production.

Television started growing as a parallel industry with cinema which saw huge migration in the limited space available. Many of the film production houses monopolized the television space and time slots and feed them with their own television productions thereby narrowing down the space for new comers as most of the content providers have their fixed and regular groups of people working for them round the clock in various departments. A direct entry in such groups for new directors and technicians is not less than breaking strong barriers erected at the entry points. The only way out to cross such hurdles is to start working from the scratch in the productions till you are able to create your own network for further growth but it is not as easy as it seems to be. A graduate from a film school may not be able to compromise with his conscience to work as a subordinate at the lowest level where he knows that cinematic knowledge and creative competence of the people above him may be nowhere near him but he has to obey their dictates besides being lowly paid for doing chattel jobs as an assistant where they may not have enough experience. It is a very humiliating and suffocating situation for a person with self respect. Even this may not be a cake walk for anybody due to interference of Trade unions who force a production house to engage their registered members only. In this complex situation the only way is to make your own films or television programs where you are the boss if one has competency and reach to a bank balance to support his cause. This may sound to be a pessimistic view however it is not so grim as many qualified people coming out of cinema schools have occupied quite a large space in the industry in almost all the departments of film making where a new comer from a film school is not only respected but also given opportunity to share his creative ideas with others. It allows him not only to be acquainted with the tricks of the trade but also helps him enlarging his own network that may come handy whenever it is required by him. For those who have not been fortunate enough to step in to any film school associating with somebody as an assistant opens up a door to realize their dreams with learning and earning simultaneously.

Team management:

It has been explained earlier that the job of a Director is not restricted to technical execution but also involves his participation and contribution in Production plan, Financing, Distribution, Exhibition, Promotion and publicity and above all business strategy. It is for this reason a Director is also called a *'film maker'* which includes his personal repo with his team members. During the production it is the director's responsibility to create a congenial working atmosphere and cooperative attitude between all the production people. Sometimes he has also to work as a *'conflict manager'* in case of any dispute and difference of opinion between people or groups. It facilitates him to obtain the best creative contribution from everybody.

The Director must take his creative unit into confidence and share his ideas about the scene and what he expects from them. While having such discussion the director should have his concept clear and must not gloat in confusion otherwise his team members won't be able to assimilate his thoughts in their contribution. This confusion will percolate to everybody.. With my own experience I can say that smaller unit as possible, is better for functional convenience and coordination for the director. This rule is very essential for a documentary film production for various reasons including the budget however it may not be that small in a fiction film due to involvement of many departments but director should try to make it as lean as he can.

Sometimes a director with little technical knowledge expects his team members to overlook and compensate his weaknesses in the production. It is possible that he completes the film with the support of his technical team but mostly such films are no more than a bundle of confusion andcontradictions. Such directors are neither able to make a good film nor are respected by his crew, in fact they are often ridiculed. Opposite to it, some time wide knowledge of a director becomes an impediment in his amicable communication with his technical members as he expects them to translate his vision and imagination as it is . He is very rigid in his concepts and does not want to shift a bit. This attitude smacks of his dictatorial attitude and arrogance. He does not like others to comment and interfere in what he has so meticulously worked out. Sometimes it so happens that a director accepts what is advised by his team mates due to respect and humanitarian grounds that may not be correct. Both these situation are not in the interest of a film therefore the director should avoid any attribute of dictatorship and compromise. The director should listen to their opinions and also appreciate if they are better than his vision. This encourages and inspires everybody to synthesize with director's ideas and they work to make it better if they can.

Director's cooperative attitude works as glue to his team mates who in turn create a bond with him for long term relationship besides creating more trust and respect for each other. It helps him to execute his vision more efficiently. A director is just not a film maker but a Manager too. He should develop proficiency in better management processes by understanding other's mind & merits and mould himself to deal with them accordingly .

XXXXX

'Motion picture is a grand art that uses elements from all other art forms. So if you consider literature, photography, music as arts, then you would have to consider filmmaking an art as well because they are all integrated.'

Scene 4:
The film art

'Cinema is a strong medium of artistic expressions'. As is generally believed, 'a moving image is thousand times more effective than a million written words.' Therefore cinema becomes an effective tool to communicate about many of the social issues. It has been successfully used to meet such social obligations. Cinema cannot be restricted to merely a means to entertain people but can be effectively utilized to inform and educate them. Like any art form Cinema is also influenced by what happens in the society and around the world where people have different opinions on a particular issue. Cinema thus becomes a form of *'interaction'* between the interested groups or individuals. Earlier when it did not gain importance there were many art forms to communicate creatively such as literature, theatre, painting, music, songs and dances etc. Cinema extended an opportunity to all these art forms to integrate and interact with people in the most creative, interesting and entertaining manners. This gave rise to many cinematic genres with a different purpose to thrive. While the most common genre of fiction films has always remained most popular, other genres too cropped up to fulfill variety of social objectives like Information, education, advertisement and promotion etc. Few enthusiastic film makers started experimenting with cinematic grammar and made experimental films like an artist would make an abstract painting. The concept of canvas painting has been extended to make Animation or cartoon films with a series of drawings giving an illusion of movement.

Fiction films:

The urge to be entertained has always been there in the back of human mind since the time immemorial. They devised various forms of entertainment and creative expressions from music to dance, drama, sporting activities, celebration of different occasion and events in life, writing, painting, sculpting, photography etc. Cinema, the moving images, was an extension of still photography. The silent films of Lumiere brothers and others which brought a revolution in cinematic expression in decades to come were a major discovery in the field of entertainment. While the initial cinema was based on reality , it did not take many years to adapt itself to the ancient form of entertainment like drama, music, songs and dances, mythological and social stories. In its raw form the silent cinema started filming live the popular stage plays with the captions in between the acts to communicate and move the story forward.

The evolution of cinema is also the evolution of *'planned cinema'* where a story is selected, screenplay written and shooting is done as planned. The technological revolution too played a very significant role to enhance on screen experience from increasing the size of cinema screen to the stereophonic or Dolby sound recording systems. Celluloid projection gave way to digital projection with flawless visual quality. Single screen cinema halls transformed to small and cozy mini theatres with maximum comforts for the audience.

The story telling in fiction films too changed many folds from melodramatic clichés to normal life experiences. Fiction films evolved two distinct patterns, one to cater to general entertainment and other for stirring the intellect of a target audience. They were later defined and identified as **'commercial films'** and **'Art films'/parallel cinema'**. They both have their distinct style of production and presentation. While commercial films are meant to earn money, the Art films take up issues related to the society and the humanity at large. Gradually the line between a commercial and an art film blurred with the changing tastes and intellectual levels of audiences.

Non- fiction Films:

The beginning of twentieth century saw a new medium of moving Images that later came to be known as 'Cinema'. It generated equal interest and excitement from film makers to film goers. It was an extension of still photography. It captured live actions with a camera capturing about 16 frames /second which looked 'live' when projected on a film screen in the same speed. The pioneers Lumiere Brothers produced their first cinema in the year 1895 by capturing 'Arrival of a train', 'Workers coming out of a factory' and many more. Thereafter other film makers like DW Griffith, Eisenstein, Edwin s Porter came in to the scene and experimented with new methodology and technology to further the impact of cinema. This discovery also generated lot of interest among people to know more about Places, countries, events etc. If we ponder in the history of cinema we come to know that the films made during the initial years were all *nonfiction* or *actuality films.*

such films were mainly based on the live coverage of real events like coronation ceremonies, Places of interest, News events, Views and opinions etc. These films were a visual documentation of reality that's why they were named as **Documentary films**. In the coming years these documentary became an important means to preserve the history of a country or a civilization in the celluloid format. In most of the countries their visual history is still preserved in film archives to keep further generations abreast of the past glory and achievements, the struggle and turmoil of their country.

During the course of time Nonfiction films have developed many other forms to cater to different purpose. News reels, Biographies, scientific research and innovations, Research and development, Promotion and publicity, Information, education and training etc became the order of the day for film makers to choose a film form to suit their requirement. In a way all these films are an offshoot of Documentary films except few differences in their treatments. Some activist film makers make documentary films to highlight the issues plaguing the society and to protest against certain policies perused by the government. Like any other medium, film also has its grey areas when some anti social groups start making provocative films to create unrest and divide in the society on the lines of region and religion, bigotry, cast and creeds or to thrust and propagate their individual opinions. The nonfiction also gives ample leg room to film makers to experiment with different ideas and vision.

Non fiction film making in general and documentary films in particular are considered to be tougher than to make fiction films. It is because documentary films are not based on a predefined story or screenplay. The concept is generated from the seed of an idea that keeps on growing and changing with the research, information received from various resources and film makers' new vision and perception during the thought process. In fact there cannot be a final screen play for a documentary film. Many times what is written in the script is not possible to shoot on location and the same cannot be recreated as documentary films are based on *'actuality'*. It is believed that all the technical departments in the production of a fiction film must be excellent while for a documentary film it is the director who must be excellent as other technical qualities here are not as important as the presentation of an idea. In a fiction film the director is the captain of the ship while in a documentary Director's imagination is the key. A documentary film maker recreates the scenes within the limits of 'reality' but staging the same has the potential to kill it.

Advertisement films:

With the growth of consumerism, competition and industrialization a need was felt to reach out to the people with the information about products and the services at their disposal. The manufacturers of goods and service providers realizing the effectiveness of moving images embarked aggressively to the production of advertisement films that are released simultaneously along with the feature films in cinema halls and the television. Gradually advertising has become an industry in itself. Corporate houses earmark a fixed budget for their annual advertizing activities. There came directors with specialization in marketing who know the pulse of their consumers and try all the tricks of the trade to induce and confuse the common men. These advertisement films hit the psyche of gullible people to make a purchase decision. The success of an advertisement film is measured through how many people are influenced by it. This is reflected in the account books of the company.

Serials and Sequels:

In the adolescent age of the cinema when the technology was not so developed, the events or a story could not be filmed at stretch and were exhibited to the audience in a closed hall on weekly basis in bits and pieces. . In such a situation the story was divided in many parts and every part was released separately week after weeks in a series. Every episode was an extension of the last one and in such manners the story progressed. The current format of television serials can be credited to be inspired by the series of scenes filmed and released in early years. Where a story is serialized and every episode takes the story further. Fictions or nonfiction television programs which run more than the required duration/length of the telecast time or single release slots, can be made in to a *'series'*.

The trend of making *'sequels'* which has long been very popular in the west has taken its roots in Indian cinema too where feature films are made in number of sequels and are released separately. The programs which can be telecast within the fixed time slots and are complete in its specific content in a single episode can be telecast any time however a series has to have a fixed and regular time slot otherwise its 'variable telecast time' will lose its continuity, purpose and interest of the audience who dedicatedly are glued to their television at a regular and convenient schedule.

Animation Films:

Unlike the films shot in 24-25 frames /second which is the running speed of the camera (The standard speed for film camera is 24 frames while for digital it is 25 frames/second) the animation camera runs on *'single frame exposure'* at a time shooting a series of still drawings or caricatures which have inherent continuity of movements in their characters/objects.

One might have noticed in a film stripe which have number of still photo frames and every frame or a photo has some action. When the same is projected in normal speed we observe an illusion of continuous action. In live shooting all the actions are recorded in normal speed of 24 frames /second while in Animation or cartoon films every action is shot in single frame. When the animated film is projected in normal speed we see a continuous action created in each drawing or a caricature.

Creating animation on celluloid is very complicated and time consuming as an artist has to draw hundreds of drawings manually which means he has to create 24 designs for a second of film time therefore preparing thousands of designs for an animation film of few minutes is not a mean task. Dozens of artistes are engaged for making these sketches, caricatures or designs. It takes months or years to make a full length animation film. These designs are prepared on transparent cell papers. Every character is drawn in separate sheets of designs and every design must have some movement of the character. There are separate designs for the background which also requires having some actions/ movement such as movement of the tree leafs in the forest.

Now of course with digital technology animation can be created faster in computers. In fact Animation has taken multiple leaps and revolutionized animation techniques which did not remain confined to just drawings and caricatures but has expanded to create special effects.

In fact the special effects created by digital technology have become an independent genre in filmmaking and gave way to produce fiction and nonfiction predominantly with special effects. While the computer animation has eased out the labor of the artistes, the process has more or less remained the same except that the designs can be prepared and action of the characters can be created in computers faster than the manual ones. The special effects and computer animation has become an inseparable ingredient of any film or television production and also revolutionized the *'action'* in cinema.

Film types and the Gauge:

The film stripe which records visuals is separated by its various **'Gauge'**. The normal film which is played in cinema hall is of 35 mm gauge which is a general standard practiced all over the world. The 70 mm film is normally a blow up version of 35 mm. The *'Blow up'* is done through an optical machine during the printing process. For smaller audience in a small auditorium of educational institutions and touring cinemas 16mm or 8mm film gauge is more accessible and convenient. A 65mm film is suitable for special effects or special screenings in IMAX or Show scan.

There is a little difference in the *'sprockets'* (the holes on both sides of the film) of a 35mm positive and 35mm negative film. These sprockets work as a grip on the machine's wheels that take it forward. Lesser gauge of film can be converted to a higher gauge by *'blow up technique'* and vice versa by reduction by an optical printer however the photographic quality in the process takes a beating to certain extent due to split of grains.

Some Raw stock manufacturers have come out with 'special film' which balances the lighting conditions including the available light as per the requirement of the director. There are separate types of film stock of different speeds to expose in various lighting conditions for indoor and outdoor shootings and for night shooting when light is very less. The selection of film stock is done by the cameraman as required in the scene.

With the technological revolution in cinema now film is fast being replaced by 'Digital technology'.   There are digital equipments available for the entire gamut of film making from cinematography to recording, editing to animation and special effects. Digital format is not only easy on the budget but also saves lot of time and space occupied by film tins, transportation cost and convenience of playing in cinema halls through digital projectors. The immediate fall out of digital revolution in cinema has been in the closure of many single screen theatres, processing film laboratories and above all the diminishing demand of raw film which has grossly affected the film manufacturers around the world.

Though celluloid film is still used for making release prints, their numbers have fallen drastically. With multiplexes coming up in every small or a big town the demand for Digital copy of the film has tremendously increased. It has also facilitated the producer to release their film in more number of screens than earlier due to saving in exorbitant print and transportation costs. Now the films can directly be beamed through internet and screened in the theatres and on television. While reducing the overall production cost of the film the digital technology has also opened new avenues for revenue generation.

Cinematography:

The word cinematography comes from the Greek roots *kinema* (movement) and *graph* (writing). A good cinematographer does more than merely light a scene or move the camera. He studies the script and creates an elaborate lighting setup and camerawork that provokes emotions and strengthen the plot. He communicates a character's dream, hope, despair, or joy based on where camera and lights are placed.

The director of photography is often called a painter and his canvas is the screen. His "brush" are the actors, the lights, the location, the set, the props, etc. These are the elements the DP can control to make each and every *shot*. The shot is the *smallest unit* of the film, the building blocks if you call, some can be small while others can be big. It's how these pieces are combined that matter.

Let us remember that movies are not plays. The power of cinematography consists of evoking emotions of delight, sadness, humor, and fear through the mastery of a cinematic syntax that has been developed for more than a century. Shot sizes, angles and movements are the heart of an exceptional camerawork, which, combined with a lighting crafted to enhance emotions, form the essence of cinematography.

The Sound in cinema :

Just imagine seeing a film without sound then you will understand the importance of sound in our life. Let's have an experiment to prove this point, shut your eyes. It is dark everywhere, you only hear ambience sounds around but can't make out what's exactly happening there. You hear drum beats, horns of cars and vehicles, people shouting, a continuously ringing bell from a distance cross your ears, a car stops with screeching sound and there is commotion. You may not be able to understand and relate sounds with specific happenings. You don't know what's the drum beat about, why a continuous bell passed across you, you are not able to identify the type of vehicles passing on the road, you are not aware of the reasons why a car stopped with screeching break sound, you don't know why people are clapping and shouting . Now close your ears for few minutes and look around. You will see traffic moving on the road, there is fight between two persons; a teenage is displaying a stunt, a car collided with another one breaking its windshield, the glass pieces are scattered on the ground etc. All this happens but you don't hear corresponding sounds of the events as if they take place silently. It makes no impact on you. Now open your eyes and ears and see. you hear vehicular sounds when traffic moves, you can identify the vehicles, you hear drum beats when the young boy is doing his stunts and people clap to appreciate him, you hear people shouting to stop a fight between two men. These not only have clear impact on you but you also understand the meaning of events. This experiment justifies the relations between visuals and sounds in our daily life. We also understand that without any one of them the life will be meaningless.

The sound in a film is as important as visuals. They complement each other. The ambience sounds and the dialogues of a scene are heard through the sound recorded and synchronized with visuals. Without sound the scene remains incomplete and ineffective. As the film technology developed the techniques of sound recording too did not leg behind. With the use of specific sounds special impact can be created in the scene. The sound is recorded simultaneously with the shooting of the visuals. While this sound may not be finally used due to its poor quality and noise disturbances, the same is used for editing as *'pilot' track.* This pilot track helps editor to synchronize dialogues and other sounds with the shots for making the rough cut of the film. *'Rough Cut'* is the first impression of a complete film. Once it is finalized all the sounds used in the film including dialogues and sound effects are dubbed and rerecorded to obtain a clean sound track.

Sound is recorded in the following methods during the shoot-

1.**Single system recording-** This is done by a single camera that records both visuals and the sound simultaneously. In this process sound is recorded in the form of magnetic or optical sound modulations on one side of the film stripe or tape. This process is in practice for recording of live events, news reporting, interviews etc for the television. The irregularity and indiscipline during the shoot has been the drawback of this system but it was useful for a **'one man unit'** where there was no other helping hand nearby. Now the sound is recorded in the similar process though digital camera, mobile phones and other digital devices.

2. **Double system recording-** In this system visuals and the sound is recorded separately however the speed of the

camera and the recorder is maintained for perfect synchronization. This process is normally used for shooting fiction films where two separate units for shooting visual and sound recording are engaged. The Camera and the recorder are interconnected to maintain the standard film speed of 24 frames/ second. In this system a recordist enjoys more functional independence to experiment with sound quality and effects. During the shoot sound is recorded on magnetic tapes while film is shot on celluloid thereafter while the picture negative is sent to laboratory for developing and printing , the sound on tape is transferred on optical sound film for editing . To facilitate the perfect synchronization of sound and picture, a clap board with all the details of the shot written on it, is clapped. This information is also recorded aurally before the clap. This helps the editor to segregate the relevant picture and the dialogues of the scene. Editor marks the clap sound on the sound track and matches it with the closure of the clap board in the picture stripe. This process is repeated with all the shots individually as per the chronological order of the script. These days' *Digital plate'* is used for synchronization. The sound modulations are recorded simultaneously on optical film as well as on magnetic tape, parallel matching of these clap points give perfect synchronization. It is very important to ensure that film and sound are recorded in the same speed otherwise it will not be possible to synchronize them. In the state of non synch the dialogues don't match with the lip movements of the characters. The non synchronization is more disturbing in close or mid shots than in long shots.

Many times multiple camera set up is used during the shooting while sound is recorded only by one recording unit or many different sounds are used in a single shot. They are recorded by multiple recording units but only one clap is used with the information of the shot. This is done to have proper co-ordination of camera and sound units in a single shot. It also helps editor to sort out relevant sounds and visuals of the corresponding shot. Sometimes it becomes difficult to interconnect the entire camera and sound recording units to run in the same standard speed therefore concerned technicians should take care to ensure that they all run in the same speed. There is no need to have synchronized shooting where there is nil or very little synchronization of picture and sound. For such shots **wild recording** can be done. 'Wild recording' means that recorder is not connected with camera however it should be running in the standard speed. Generally sound effects are recorded wild. To achieve perfect synchronization the most popular technique is **'crystal synch'**. In this technique synchronization is obtained through pendulum like movement of a crystal which is fixed in every device. In another technique the real time is coded in film and the tape which is called **'Time code'** that helps to get perfect synchronization. In addition, regulating a **'synch pulse'** fitted in camera and the recorder also helps in flawless synchronization.

The job of a recordist is to record noiseless and clear sounds that are heard in **'the take'** including dialogues and effects. Back ground narrations, special sound effects, back ground music etc may be recorded later. For **the** best quality of sounds during the shoots the recordist must ensure proper placement of microphones, sound levels and mixing of various sound indicators in the recorder. No one expects an excellent sound quality at this stage, excellence can be achieved by the recordist later during the dubbing, back ground music recording, effect recording and ultimate **re-recording** (mixing). Recordist must maintain a record of sounds on a prescribed form of *'dope sheet'* that are important for ambience and continuity including non synchronous effects in the shots.

Post shoot activities including editing and recording generally consume more time and efforts than the shooting itself. It is the stage the sound requirement for the scene is designed while editor is editing the film. The rough cut is prepared that presents an overall picture and the requirement of sounds to enhance the impact of the scenes are worked out. In this effort editor and director are available to advise the recordist and provide suggestions accordingly. At this stage sometimes special recording sessions are staged and sound recreated to have fine quality of sound tracks. Pre recorded sound effects too become handy when it is not possible to record them in the studio.

Film Appreciation:

Understanding or appreciation of cinema is another vital factor in the process of film making. Film appreciation is the analysis of the technical quality, effectiveness of narration; assessment the success quotient and impact of the film on audience. It is not necessary that a film critic must be a film expert like a film director because film appreciation requires a neutral assessment of its overall impact it makes on a viewer who may not necessarily be a film buff. Since cinema is a combination of various art forms it is not required for a filmgoer to have the knowledge of any art forms. The purpose of audience when they go to watch a movie is mostly to entertain however the criteria for an entertainment may differ from person to person, therefore the Film critic analyses the factors which could interest the audience in general or a target group in particular for whom the film is made. Film appreciation ,criticism or a review is more an opinion of an individual that may not be similar to others. Every opinion on a film may vary depending on the personal choice of subjects, liking and disliking and interest of the person who reviews it. Sometimes the reviews are influenced by the personal association of the writer with the stake holders, allurements and obligations etc. There has come a new phenomenon of paid Film appreciation or reviews to boost up the chances for higher revenue collection or to sabotage a rival's film. In the days of stiff competition at the limited exhibition windows such tactic are employed by the scared rivals.

The commercial success of a film depends on the impact it creates on the viewers and acceptability of the audience not merely for its technical quality but for its overall impression it leaves on people. It is also not necessary that a film must be technically excellent for its success. Many times its narration leaves an everlasting impact over their viewers that makes the film a commercial success. The background and the upbringing of the audience also play an important role for its success therefore there cannot be rigid parameters for a person who reviews a film. A film academician will appreciate a film on its technical quality, its story telling, behavior of the characters, analyzing the situations and over all flow of the film etc. A common man will judge a film according to his liking and disliking and influence of stars working in the film , actions etc. A critic who is generally an opinion maker may comprehend technical quality as well as the story and the narration, performance of various departments etc. It is also possible that a technically excellent and well made film may not go down the throat of people in the cinema hall but the same film may earn the tag of a classic or a cult film. Generally weekly appreciation and reviews of films appearing in regular film columns are personal views of the writers who could be anybody from a journalist to an educationist or an activist to a film maker whose opinions matter as they are regularly read by people. The reviews have developed the potential to make or mar the success of a film at the ticket windows however these reviews are very important for film buffs and students of cinema.

XXXXX

'If a Film is well made and successful, it is everyone's credit but if it is bad, lacks standard and quality, unsuccessful to attract people to the ticket counters then it is the Director's failure.'

Scene 5:
The Production Strategy

The problem faced in a production is not that of dearth of a story , the format or the clarity and understanding of the director about the subject but most usually it is lack of planning, prior preparations and resources etc. Excluding the corporate or an established production house' involvement in the productions, in most of the cases there is just one or two persons who alternate as both the producer and the director when a decision is taken to produce a film without support of a dependable unit at this stage. The producer himself has to work on the planning and make preparations. In the absence of a detailed plan before shoots if it is not impossible, it is very difficult to proceed further. When there is a single individual dons two hats of a producer and the director on his head, things are bit more complicated.

 If a person acts only as a Producer he has to find out a director who can deliver the film of his choice whether it is a commercial film or an art film. The selection of a director is to be made very carefully by considering his interest. A director may not be comfortable to make an action film or another may not be suitable for an emotional subject. Similarly an art film maker may not compromise with his ideas of presenting a film as realistic as possible or a commercial director may not risk making an art film. It also happens that a director who has been working with high cost productions or for established banners may not prefer to be restricted in a shoe string budget where he has to work hard to meet various ends. The selection of a director is done by the producer according to the type of film he wants to make, the finance and other resources available to him. Generally a director must be selected before a story is finalized so the director is also in loop to select a story that suits his taste.

The moment a director is selected, the first and foremost task is to find out a suitable story before chalking out a plan. The importance of a good story and developing the same to an interesting screenplay cannot be undermined. There are many more jobs that are to be accomplished under the direct supervision of the producer and director jointly. These tasks cannot be left to the discretion of other people or the unit members, technical experts or the departments. In fact even if a producer has a reliable group of people around him he should not shut his eyes to the happenings around. Therefore it is imperative for a producer-director to accomplish the preliminary tasks of selecting a story, a writer, budgeting, broad outline of the project plan ,probable idea about the cast within his budget suitable to their liking and the interest. Whether it is small budget or a high budget film or a television production there is mostly no supporting unit in place initially which is likely to be not possible too soon due to financial reasons. Many times producer- director don't have an office to perform routine official activities such as telephones, typing and copying, dispatch of letters, hospitality and entertainment of guests which are to be carried out by him. In the production of fiction films support of an Art director can be sought however for non fiction films, everything has to be done by the producer-director himself. Besides the financial crunch there is another reason for such crisis that the non fiction films are the outcome of the figment of imagination of the director only as there can be no role for an exclusive screen play writer for such films. In my opinion the script for the non fiction film should always be written by a director. In case of a research oriented and specialized subject the services of an expert consultant can be obtained . Most of the documentary films are an extension of an idea and there can be no fixed and clear concept of subject matter, chronology of scenes and final shape of the film. So the director himself works out an outline of the film instead of depending on others to guide him , write a concept or the script for him as it may be difficult to synthesis with the ideas of another person who will have his own independent thinking. Even if it is done then the director of a documentary or a nonfiction film will become a mere visual translator of the script handed over to him. In this case the director's vision, imagination and the creativity in the film will be absent.

It is very taxing for an individual to shoulder the entire responsibility of producing a fiction film alone therefore the moment money is arranged for the project the producer must engage a reliable Production manager or an Associate Producer at the earliest. An office secretary to handle day to day activities in the office to take care of the phone calls, networking, typing and dispatching of the letters or mails, guest entertainment etc should be next in the line of engagements. Other tasks on priority include screen play writing, budgeting, , engagements of technical crew members, selection of artistes, obtaining   permission for shoots on locations and   the studios, preparation of costumes and set designing, property, hiring of equipments etc. No shoots should be started without foolproof shooting arrangements to avoid last minute hitches.

Financial discipline:

No amount of money is enough for film making whether it is a low budget or a high budget film. If there is limited finance the director has to work under strict financial discipline within the budgetary provisions therefore the director must practice the policy of **'cheap and the best'** to find out an efficient team and the most economical alternatives to shoot a scene without compromising on its final outcome. In case if the cost of shoots increases, the director must work on alternative scenes including rewriting to reduce the cost. Cost can be saved for example, by hiring the costumes instead of getting stitched for every character when there is no continuity. Many art film makers of realistic films request the actors to bring their own dresses and deposit them with the costume department till the shoot is over or one can buy readymade dresses as and when required for continuity. Similarly number of sets or the scenes (by merging with other), short length of the takes (instead of lengthy and complicated shot takings), the total number of days of the shooting, number of junior artists can be reduced to minimum.

If the film is being shot in celluloid format the requirement of raw stock (unexposed picture negative) may be curtailed by reducing the **'exposed ratio'**. An 'exposed ratio' is the ratio between the total length and the exposed quantity of the film. It entails a very significant expenditure and can save lot of money on account of the cost of the raw material and the laboratory expenses. Selection of the locations can be done in such a way that most of them are in close periphery to save money in shifting the locations, transportation and accommodation etc . Such financial disciplines can be taken care of at the time of writing itself. Suggestions to shoot in huge sets and costly locations must be avoided at any cost for a low budget film.

Having excess money also is not without troubles and complications. This happens with very high budget films where distributors and the exhibitors insist on casting big stars for every character and the poor director is haunted by the uncertainties and insecurities of having such a set up. Producer and director have to dance to the whims and the fancies of these stars whose inflated ego is so fragile that no one knows when they will be hurt. Many big films are stuck in between due to conflict with actors. In case it is completed at all then there are problems in its release. Release dates have to consider many factors like no other star film should be released simultaneously; it should be released in a weekend with many holidays or the festivals taking place. The exhibitors too play hard balls with the distributors to extract their pound of flesh from the star cast films. There are always watchful eyes of anti social elements, smugglers, dons and mafia watching the fate of a big film and its success brings with it more insecurity for its stars, producers and the director. There are cases when there have been extortion calls, murders and kidnappings of people associated with these films. These are few factors that restrict Indian cinema, which produces maximum number of film annually, to find a place in the world.

The problems faced by small budget films are not due to ample money available but the lack of it. This can be sorted out by the proper coordination between a producer and the director. cost cutting measures may be incorporated in the script therefore it is necessary to write a detailed screen play before shoot is started. Last minute changes in the script , anticipating the problems during the shoots, mismanagement of time and shooting schedules,, technical glitches in the equipments etc may be avoided. A careful and meticulous planning saves a lot of stress , energy and the efforts of the producer and the director that ultimately is reflected in the final outcome of the film.

Selection of crew:

It is the primary responsibility of the producer to engage the technicians and other crew members in consultation with the director with in the budgetary provisions for the same. In low budget film director should explore meritorious newcomers who have attained proficiency and speed in their field. Such people may be derived from film schools, assistants in various fields who have long experiences and are looking for an opportunity to prove them. Speed of execution of the respective jobs is one of the main criteria for selection of these people as a small budget producer cannot afford a slow and snarling speed of work. Sometimes suggestions may also be received from financiers and distributors for the preference of a particular person which is not a normal practice. A producer is free to choose his team with in his budget. Where the person works as producer and the director he has to take his own decisions.

While in small budget film ,merit and speed of the technicians is the deciding factor, in high budget production established people with proven records are preferred. Their credentials should be impeccable and undoubted. Sometimes corporate houses and stars of the film have their preferences of the technicians which is difficult for a producer to ignore. It normally happens in case of cameraman.

In the earlier years of cinema when the films were produced by studios technicians and main crew members were engaged on monthly remuneration. In such arrangements director was bound to work with these people .He had no choice to bring his trusted technicians .Many problems in this system were automatically sorted out but coordination between the director and his team members were not easy to accomplish as they were not answerable to the Director but to the studio which had engaged them. The director had to make an extra effort to achieve and create a congenial working atmosphere. With the gradual closure of studios the coordination became much easier between the director and his team. But the studio system has bounced back in different form with the growth of television and production of daily or weekly soaps where requirement of a regular team made it imperative to have people on salary. This system has its own advantages as the technicians or the actors in many cases don't have to struggle for another assignment till the series is telecast. In most of the cases the life of a series is longer than expected based on its TRPs.

The director must prefer only those people who have the capacity, capability, resourcefulness and the merits to understand his vision and imagination .They should be able to translate his vision and concept on the screen. The director should avoid engaging people only because of personal connections, relations and affiliations. Such people may not have the desired merit. The first and foremost important selection is that of a cameraman who not only has to win the trust of the director but also of the actors. The cinematography in a film plays an important role in showcasing the beauty on the screen including glamorizing the locations and the actors. A beautifully photographed film works as an eye candy for the viewers and has the potential to camouflage many inherent flaws of the film.

The next most important appointment is that of an Editor whose sense of vision and imagination along with the sense of cutting contributes great deal in making or damaging a film. In fact the editing of the film must starts from the time of writing the screenplay. While a director may have a good sense of editing the contribution of an editor in cutting and experimenting with frames only provides a shape, speed and the continuous flow to the film. It may be noted that an editor with a vision can cut a film in number of styles giving different impact to the scene and a choice to the director to choose one of them however sometimes such experiments may be in conflict with the concept of the director. In such a situation the director must be very clear about his requirements of pace, movement and impact of the film/scene and communicate to the editor accordingly. This clarity of his vision must also reflect in his shot takings. This makes an editor's job easy otherwise slow moving Shots cannot look natural when cut in fast speed. During the shoots the director must maintain a consistent and uniform movement speed in accordance with the flow of the story.

Timing:

Time element or the *'timing'* in a scene makes it more effective or less effective. The effect of the scene lingers in people's memory for longer time than the scene itself. Slow moving scene does not require much of editing while fast moving scenes like action sequences not only need fast cutting but also need placement of the shots effectively so that action sustains the interest of the audience till the end. The length of the shots in action is shorter than the dialogue or emotional scenes therefore director must work out the tempo of the scene and decide the length of each shot accordingly. The timing also includes the total length or the duration of the scene which will remain on the screen. Unduly longer or a shorter length of the scene impacts in its narrative and it outcome. While deciding the length of a scene director should maintain the overall pace of the film otherwise ping pong of slow and fast scenes will create more jerks and obstructions in the film.

Normally when a director or a producer is involved actively in the writing of screen play, he loses the neutrality of judgment and is not in a position to take a call on what is to be deleted, retained or modified during the editing stage and is not ready to accept what the editor edits. It creates conflict of interest among them. Many times these disputes are related to the timing, tempo and pace of the film therefore the director must maintain a neutral stance and be objective and not interfere in editor's job at least till the rough cut of the film is ready .It gives an opportunity to the editor to give his best. After seeing the rough cut director and editor together may discuss and come to a common solution and modify the editing pattern if required. Neutrality also helps the director to take an objective approach at a later stage when he has come out of the attachment of the script and may find many things in the screenplay irrelevant.

Pace:

The success of a film depends to a large extent on its **'Pace'** and the interest retained from the beginning till end. The director who is able to conceive his film from the view point of his audience before the start of the shoots is on the road to success. He should clearly know what would appeal to his audience and what would put them off. Every scene of the film must leave a long lasting impression in his mind so that whenever he discusses it with others it runs like a film in front of him. The pace of the film should synthesize with the mood of the scenes.

No director wants to make a bad film however it becomes one when it is completed without him being aware of it. It becomes difficult to find out flaws in his film and to know what his audience did not accept. The likes and dislikes of the viewers depend on the following factors-

1.Screen play- Before writing the screenplay the director has to decide if he wants to make a comedy film or a serious one, high speed action film or a slow moving emotional film, every scene is developed keeping in mind the interest and acceptability by the audience. Some group of people like youngsters prefer to enjoy a fast paced film but seniors and older people like to enjoy an emotional drama therefore while writing the script director must consider the interest of such groups.

2.Casting- Director must select the cast which is suitable to his characters. Wrongly cast film is a sure disaster. A comedy actor may not impress in serious roles or vice versa. Image of an actor is a permanent brand for the audience and they may not like to fiddle with it so while casting a particular actor his image in the audience should be taken care off. Beside it director must ensure whether a particular actor who is being cast would be able to play certain scenes which may be different than his broad image or his performance capabilities.

Sometimes it may happen that a comedy actor may also perform equally in better in serious roles but it may not be the case with others. The films like *'Asoka the Great'* by *Sivan* and *'Devdas'* of *sanjay Bhansali* made with a very high budget have suffered due to their wrong choice of main characters while a low budget *'Chandni Bar'* made by *Madhur Bhandarkar* was a huge success because Tabboo very aptly chosen for the role of a Bar dancer in this film.

3.Production design- It means that every detail of the screen play, further requirements and arrangements are properly enumerated and worked out for every scene including color scheme, emotional impact, set and property requirements etc. This not only makes every one's job easy but also creates a clear understanding of director's needs to enable them work within the set parameters and restrictions.

It is very common with big budget films having top stars that scenes are changed to the liking and disliking of star performers. Here it is more a compulsion for a director than his willingness to make such thoughtless modifications. Such changes disturb the entire concept and impact of the film including its pace that obstructs a continuous flow beside incurring extra expenditure to incorporate them. It should never become a habit of the director to indulge in last minute changes whether it is a low budget or a high budget film.

4.Shooting Ratio- It is the ratio between the total exposed material (Raw stock/ exposed film or digital material) and the final film in terms of its length or duration. The director should have complete control on this ratio as increase in ratio increases the cost. An experienced director generally with meticulous planning is able to keep it under control.

Sometime during the shooting of a documentary , a live event, an action scene or with the use of multiple cameras, it is difficult to restrict the exposed ratio as such shooting cannot be planned efficiently and director experiences a little control over the events and the raw stock. Though such exigencies make a difference in the budget director must foresee such eventualities and make budgetary provisions for the same.

High budget films are shot in magnanimous sets, foreign locations, with hundreds of junior artistes and high voltage action sequences using multiple cameras as a practice. Though there may not be any restrictions on shooting ratio,it is negligible in high project cost. In low budget films cost of raw stock takes a significant chunk of the expenditure therefore ratio restrictions must be imposed strictly. This can be achieved by an experienced director easily with prior rehearsals of the scenes however lack of director's experience may bring the producer to the brink of bankruptcy. The normal shooting ratio should be 4:1 which can vary according to the requirements but in no case should go out of hand.

The control over shooting ratio particularly if the film is being shot on celluloid format is important due to the fact that raw film is an import material that has high import cost therefore in a low budget film the expenditure on this account amounts to one third or more. While working on the raw stock ratio director also takes a decision about the gauge (35mm, 16mm,70mm or cinemascope), Black & white or color. If the film is exclusively made for television it can be shot in 16mm or digital format. The shooting ratio can be relaxed when the film is being shot on video or digital format as the cost of tape is less however higher shooting ratio in any format also extends shooting duration that will have a significant increase in the cost. These factors have direct bearing on the budget.

When the shoot is done with multiple cameras, the number of cameras must be pre decided to avoid last minute confusion. It may happen that some time an additional camera is not required and it remains idle for the day, if it happens it is a reflection of director's inefficiency.

My long experience in direction tells me that a meticulous planning for a director is full of excitement, challenges and educating with new information. It helps a director to give final shape to the images he has formed in his mind and also provide him a window to have a peep over the final impact of the film. I am of the opinion that this is his first step towards the success.

XXXXX

'A plot can be construed as a single line concept of a story which needs to be developed.'

Scene 6:
The Plot

A Plot is generally perceived as a raw, desolate and uneven piece of land where any type of structure can be erected with proper concept, clarity of purpose and planning as required and imagined by the developer. Similarly in cinema a plot means a vague concept that needs to be developed to a story with proper vision and imagination of the Producer, writer and the director. **Plot** refers to the sequence of events inside a story which affects other events through the principle of cause and effect. The causal events of a **plot** can be thought of as a series of sentences linked by "***and so.***"

Examples of '*PLOT*' in a sentence:
1.Naina was mesmerized by the charm of Manu's personality when she met him after many years.

2. Anupriya lost interest in her life when she realized her mistake of not recognizing that sudeep always took care of her whenever she was in distress and needed him but it was too late.

3.The strict discipline of Col. Vishwajeet forced his only son Srijan to run away from the house to take revenge with his father.

4. Ram Chandra was not happy when he got a job in reserved quota as it undermined his own self respect and merits.

5. Dayal at the sunset of his life, was still waiting for the return of Laxmi, the women he loved and lost forever.

A *plot* can be construed as a single line concept of a story which needs to be developed. The plot, characterization, dialogues, emotions, pace and rhythm, Presentation and the production are few of many factors that directly or indirectly influence the story. It is not necessary that all these factors should be present in an average or a fixed ratio in the story content. Many times the economic compulsions of the production too decide about their ratio. In some stories emotional quotient may be dominating while in others it could be action. They all influence the basic factors of a story. Some stories may have simple characters while in others they may be difficult to deal with and understand easily. The beginning of a film could be a mix of the present or past events and situations which are relevant to the social context, period, place of incidents and beauty of the locations etc.

The Situations:

The common viewer of a film or theatre normally ignores the present situations as they are not aware of their inadvertent impact the story would make on their mind. The present situations only affect a story or the growth of characters. In the absence of present situations the characters would look groping in zero space and the audience confused. The present situations only make a character sensitive and full of feelings. They take their audience to a journey of their past and the future so the *'present'* itself becomes the present of the characters and the viewers. These situations play a covert role in the plot and weave new characters, events, stress and curiosity, twists and complications to take the story forward. These situations generate audience's acceptability of the characters and their authenticity. In these situations audience look for the period of the story, cultures and the traditions, life styles and the behavior of people and the characters, therefore the knowledge of periodic situations and circumstances, place of events, social fabrics and their cultural traditions, general Intelligence, Law and order and political back grounds, Religion and beliefs of the people etc. is essential.

Many decades ago in the year 1919 an English author *'Wycliffe A. Hill'* discovered elementary aphorisms of a story. He believed that there were only *36 maxims* to create a plot. All the stories are generally based on these formulae and have their variations.

- **Happy Situations:**

    1. Rescue
    2. Lost loved ones recovered
    3. A miracle of God

- **Pathetic situations:**

    4. Entreaty
    5. Love's obstacles
    6. Rivalry between unequal
    7. Rivalry between kinsmen
    8. A mystery

- **Inspiring situations**:

  9. Loving an enemy
  10. Sacrifice of oneself for an ideal.
  11. Sacrifice of oneself for Kindred

- **Disastrous situations precipitated without criminal intent:**

  12. Possessed of an ambition
  13. Fatal indiscretion
  14. Pursuit
  15. Rebellion
  16. Enmity between kinsmen
  17. Effort to obtain
  18. Daring effort
  19. Vengeance
  20. Kindred avenged against kindred
  21. Mistaken jealousy
  22. Involuntary criminal love

- **Disastrous situations precipitating with criminal intent:**

  23. Struggle against God
  24. Abduction
  25. To sacrifice all for a passion
  26. Adultery
  27. Adultery with murder
  28. Criminal love

- **Tragic situations over which the victim has no control:**

29. Loved ones lost
30. Falling a prey
31. Disaster
32. An innocent suspected
33. Obligation to sacrifice loved ones
34. To learn of the dishonor of the loved ones
35. Mental derangement
36. To kill a kinsmen or a friend
37. Remorse

The period:

The suggestions of *'Time'* when the events take place facilitate the audience to travel to that period immediately and they become part of that era. This *'span of the story'* extends the process of occurrence of the events in the entire plot. The span may vary from days to months and the years. In this span every event has its own period and the season of occurrence which gives it a definite identity and purpose. A film or a part of it can be designed in any specific season such as rainy, winter or the spring season if the story has specific relevance and requirements. Similarly the story may also emphasis a particular festival, occasion or the boundary.

The Dramatic Time:

The duration of an *Act* is the **'Time taken by an event or the scene of the story or the drama to travel to the next act'.** This helps to complete the entire chain of events in the story with in a limited time frame. This timing can vary from one scene to another if required. While writing the screen play every scene may be allotted some days or weeks of **dramatic duration** to maintain continuity of events.

Physical environment:

As it suggests **it is the environment, atmosphere and the ambience where the events or the action takes place**. In the narration , the physical environment of the place is detailed minutely to build up the impact of the story therefore the director must attain a thorough knowledge of the place, its history, environment and culture, society and the traditions.

The Geographical locale:

It means the country, the area, the district or the village where the story unfolds. The geographical locale can sometimes also be informed through dialogues however the emotional relationship and the impact of this in the narrative of the story must never be ignored and the writer should make full use of such provisions.

The Location:

No event or action can take place without a specified location. This physical location should by all means be decided by the director while writing the screen play however unnecessary details about the location at this stage are not required and may be avoided to give him more liberty to roam freely in his imagination and creativity to make necessary changes in the scene accordingly. The details which have the potential to enhance the effect of the scene may be included in the script.

Extending his list of common plots *Wycliffe* also listed common locations where generally a film is shot or the events take place. They are-

1.Aeroplane, 2.Ship, 3.Train, 4.Advertising agency, 5.erospace, 6.Dictator's headquarter, 7.House of dignified person, 8.Army post, 9.Artist's studio, 10.Stadium, 11.Foriegn township, 12.cotton fields, 13.Court, 14.Dance floor, 15.Shop/store, 16.Desert, 17.Shipyard, 18.Factory, 19. Farm fields, 20.Fishermen's colony, 21.Lake, 22.Advocate's chamber, 23.Light house, 24.Cattle shed, 25.Mansion, 26.Matro city, 27.Mining center, 28.Embassy. 29.Motel, 30.Police station, 31.Prison, 32.Publication house, 33.Racecourse, 34.Radio/television station, 35.Railway station, 36.Trench/Pit, 37.Bank, 38.Warfield, 39.Seaside/beach, 40.Grove, 41.Cave, 42.Broker's office, 42.Sharemarket, 43.Cabrette,Camp, 45.Forest, 46.Gamblers' den, 47.Criminals'den, 48.Playground, 49.Port, 50.Hospital, 51.Hotel, 52.Island, 53.Laboratory, 54.Film studio, 56.National Borders, 57.Newspaper house, 58.Night club, 59.Brothel, 60.Astronomical laboratory, 61.Execution home, 62.Culvert, 63.Pirates'den, 64.Gardens, 65.Rest house, 66.Rice /grain fields, 67.River, 68.Sailoon, 69.Ocean, 70.Small town, 71.Godown, 72.Stage, 73.Stock exchange, 74.Hot regions, 75.Underground activities, 76.Waterfronts, 77.Village, 78.Snowfields/places, 79.Zoo, 80.Office, 81.Hutments, 82.Chawls, 83.Dispensary, 84.Places of worship. 85.Streets, 86.Lanes/by lanes, 87.Bridges/flyovers, 88.Flowerbeds, 89.Hill stations.

The Social context:

The plot of any story or a drama revolves around various social groups around us. They may be our family and its members with whom we have intimate connection or other groups who are directly or indirectly related to our lives at various levels. All these social groups differ in their back ground, ideology, behavior, socio economic situations that give them their distinct identity and influence personality of their people. In the stories that are woven around a family, realistic situations can be portrayed around intimate relationships but in other social groups that are devoid of emotional intimacy, such portrayals may look concocted and dramatic thus make no impact. Sometimes such characters are created deliberately who do not look real for the sake of entertainment. In other social groups friendship, professional relations or based on various socio economic status, romantic liaison are important. The members of this entire group have different behavioral pattern which is reflected in the development of the characters.

1.The family:

Family comes first among all the social groupings. Everybody is connected with his mother, father, brothers, sisters and other relations. A family is the basic unit of a society which cannot be ignored by a writer. This unit of a family establishes an identity of all the characters that creates a link between them and the audience. Every person in a family has a different role to play which are the basic constituents in the growth of characters. The writer must be conscious of the sensitivities of every relationship which has to reflect in the characters.

2. Friendship:

Next to the family comes friendship which is out of the family's periphery. Friendship differs with the situations and the immediate circumstances. It has many types but the common thread between them is friendly connections. Another dimension in friendship is that of *romantic relationship* which is normally established between the persons of opposite sex. The main difference between a friendship and romantic relationship is that of *'attraction'*. It is not necessary to have an attraction and emotional link in friendship which is essential for a romantic liaison. This variation makes a difference in the development of various characters.

3. Professional:

People engaged in similar profession or institutions develop a functional relationship and expect special considerations. Everyone in such groups' works within the set parameters and discipline as in Navy, Army, Police or any other profession. Their specific behavior and personality authenticates their profession.

4.Dignitaries:

People in this group represent a special category of high end and rich in their social, economical and the political status. They give orders to the people comparatively in lower rank in education and professional strata. The difference between high and low can be easily noticed in their behavior and mannerism. People in subordination salute or wish them humbly bending forward while those in higher peddles look them with authority and arrogance. This discrimination between classes of people is the result of traditions and ethnic culture which can be easily identified with their dressings, ornaments and jewelry, language etc. This class discrimination provides a definite identity to various characters in the film.

5.Social standards:

Every society or a social group consists of some definite

traditions and behavior which is expected to be followed by everybody. This behavioral pattern is ingrained in their etiquettes. Most of the people display their personality according to their social and economic standards which confirms to their status. Any change in their behavior marks an aberration and is then protested by those who profess it. Traditionally such class differences were created by religious, political and cultural parameters but in modern times of scientific innovations and applications these cultural and religious traditions are still followed by middle class in respect of equality and law and order in the society.

6.Economic system:

The economic system created by the state effect everyone in the country irrespective of their social groupings. There are two classes of *1. The Ruler and 2. The ruled*. They have distinct identity in public and private domains. While a ruler displays his freedom of action and ideology, the ruled display signs of slavery and subordination.

7.Politics and the law:

The laws of the land are governed and enacted based on the political and legal decisions of the state. They affect every one differently therefore the writer and the director should have fairly good knowledge of the politics and the laws of the nation.

8.Intellectuals and opinion makers:

The intellectuals and the opinion makers have always been a great asset since the beginning of humanity. Their opinion provides a direction to the society by influencing the minds and beliefs of common men. This group includes Religious preachers and priests, teachers, leaders, journalists, actors and other performers etc. Their daily discourses and ideology influence day to day life of people. These intellectuals and opinion makers are the instrument in preserving the social and cultural heritance and traditions Therefore to develop such characters an extensive research is important and necessary to ensure how a character from this group will behave and how he can influence people in general.

9.Faith and beliefs:

Every society has its own religious factors, rituals, festivals and religious traditions which influence people since their birth. These faiths and beliefs not only influence their life styles but also their ideology though the intensity of influence may vary due to many social and economic factors. It is not necessary that everybody is influenced equally. It depends on the intellectual level of an individual which decides the amount of his faith and beliefs in religion and traditions. It is the reason that we see two types of people 1. *A theist* and *2. An atheist* and it is evident in their characters and behavior. It is very common these days by a group to protest against depiction of certain faiths and beliefs in the excuse of 'hurting their sentiments'. Sometimes these protests damage a film's collection.

The writer and the director must ensure that when they are developing a character from any of the above groups they must study them thoroughly as their depiction will be closely observed by the audience while they watch a film, a drama or a television serial. A wrong depiction will not only nullify their effect but also question their authenticity and make the characters hollow and laughable. This is one of the major factors of the failure of any production of film , drama or television show that concocts the situations and characters which are not natural. These things are not taught in any school but the writer and the director must learn themselves by minute observation around.

The writer must ensure while writing screen play or a drama that all his characters should have born before their entry in the script so that their character has already taken a shape and there is no need to waste time to show his growth until and unless there is a need to show the birth of a character and his subsequent growth. The past of a character shapes his present and future behavior and actions.

Wycliffe A. Hill during his research on the stories not only discovered common themes but also analyzed them to enlist common characters used in these plots. These characters consist of various socioeconomic groups drawn from different geographical backgrounds, prepare the ground for an entertaining story line.

Common characters:

These characters include- 1.Actors/Actresses, 2,Advertiser, 3.Representative, 4.Protester/Agitator, 5.Anarchist, 6.Relegious preacher, 7.Performer, 8.Astrologer, 9.Astronomer, 10.Blackmarketeer,11.Blacksmith, 12.Blind, 13.Librarian, 14.Agent/Broker, 15.Pirates, 16. Builder, 17.Tyrant, 18.Thief, 19.Quality controller/inspector, 20.Hero/Brave, 21.Priest, 22,Driver, 23.Pharmasist, 24.Microanalyst, 25.clerk, 26.Joker, 27.cobbler, 28.Funnyman/comedian, 29.Body builder/Athlete,

30.Accountant, 31.Motor racer, 32.Pilot, 33.Player, 34.Dacoit, 35.Banker/cashier, 36.Fool, 37.Prince/Ruler, 38.Begger, 39.chef,,. 40. Cannibal, 41.Wealthy, 42.Captain/Boss, 43. Forest thief, 44.Cartoonist, 45.Treasurer,Animal thief, 46.Horse rider, 47.Cavemen, 48.Socialist, 49.Conducter, 50.Trustee, 51.Leader, 52.Magician, 53.Police constable, 54.Contracter, 55.Convict, 56.Police, 57..Fraudester, 58.Shephered, 59.Disable, 60. Truthful warrior, 61.Dancer, 62.Deaf, 63.Dentist, 64.Spy, 65.Devotee, 66.Diver, 67.Divorced, 68.Legger, 69.Naughty, 70.Forecaster, 71.Gambler, 72.Criminal, 73.Jewelthief, 74.General, 75.Swordman, 76.Governer, 77.Abductor, 78.Mortgaged, 79.Hunch backed, 80.Hunter, 81.Hypnotist, 82.Inventor, 83.Invester, 84.Jailer/Prison superintendent, 85.Jweller, 86.Psychic, 87.Marine, 88.Martyr, 89.Companion, 90.Mayer, 91.Doctor, 92.Businessman, 93.Minister, 94.Miser, 95.Crowd puller, 96.Alcoholic, 97.Drug manufacturer, 98.Editor, 99.Embezzeler, 100.Expatriate.

101. Engineer, 102.Accontant, 103.Firefighter, 104.Fisherman. 105. Fraudulent, 106.Guard, 107.Guide, 108.Gunmen, 109.Vagabond, 110.Mercyless, 111.Physician, 112.Saint, 113.Highway pirates, 114. Professional riders, 115, Judge, 116.King, 117.Warrior king, chief, 118.Labourer, 119.Advocate, 120. Life savior, 121. Creditor, 122.Model, 123.Nuisence talker, 124.Killer, 125.Musician, 126.Dumb, 127.Lame, 128.Womanizer, 129.Ideal person, 130.Author/Novelist,131.Nurse,132.Officer,134.Poet,135.Singer,136.Absconder,136.Areligious, 137.Child labor, 138.Dramatist, 139. Burglar, 140hunt –thief, 141.Chairman, 142.Herdsman, 143. Wrestler, 144. Rebellion, 145.Correspondent, 146.Mariner, 147.Wild, 148.Educationist,

149. Scientist, 150.Worshipper, 151.Scout, 152.Social worker, 152.Short and fat man, 153.Steal maker, 154.Textilemaker, 155.Stenographer, 156.Homeless, 157.Rowdy, 158.Swimmer, 159.swindler, 160.Union leader, 161.Grabber, 162.Devil, 163.Vampire, 163.Brutal, 164.Indecent, 165.Throttler, 166.Guardian, 167.Soldier, 168.Watch repairer, 169.Watchman, 170.Reciever, 171.Extravagent, 172.Professor, 173.Psychologist, 173.Boxer, 174.Marine cashier, 175.Horse Trainer, 176.Horse racing coach. 177. Bribe taker, 178.Annoncer/Anchor, 179.Servant, 180.Sheriff, 181.Bishop, 182.Captain of the ship, 183. Water queen, 184.Suspicious, 185.Slave, 186.Smuggler,, 187.Tailor, 188.Skin specialist, 189.Telegrapher, 190.Telephone operator, 191.Hunter, 192.Dictator, 193.Bruital, 194.Ampire, 195.Responsible, 196.Black magician, 197.Specialist, 198.Maid servant, 199.Homemaker, 200. Student.

201. Roughen, 202.Adulterater, 203.Lover boy and girl, 204.Informer, 205.Engine driver, 206.Ticketcoleector, 207.Shoppkeeper, 208.Filmmaker, 209.Publisher, 210.Traditionalist/religious, 211.Historical, 212.Imaginative, 213.African/Negro, 214.Mangole, 215.Englishman, 216.Assistant, 217.Delivery Nurse, 218.Person who assumes various characters, 219.Crafty, 220.Washerman, 221.Coolie, 222.Women carrying water on head, 223.Carpenter, 224.Farmer, 225.Landlord, 226.Atheist.

Development of the Plot:

The development of a Plot is undertaken in following steps such as-

1. **Establishment of the Problem:** In the first step the problem and the characters are introduced in which various dimensions and contradictions of the issues are brought to the notice of the audience. The objective of this introduction is to make people start thinking about the solution but it is neither to make them aware of the issue or bring them on the same wavelength as that of the characters nor to instigate them to chase for a solution. The resolution of the problem should be revealed in layers gradually and not at a time. The beginning and the built up should not take more than $1/6^{th}$ of the total time.

Pakeeza is one of many mile stones in the history of Indian cinema. Directed by Kamal Amrohi the film has been widely appreciated for its dialogues, emotional performances, cinematography and the screenplay in which special attention had been paid to the Period, situations, country, Physical and panoramic locations.

Scene no: 1

Name of the scene: Introduction scene

Time: Night

Location: Nargis's brothel, Road

Shot 1- Crane shot, Nargis is dancing in her dance hall. Shahab enters from the main entrance in to the hall.

Monologue: 'This is Nargis, younger sister of Nawab Jaan whose husky voice and ankle bells have made the world crazy. Many hearts fall on her feet but she continues to dance without caring for them. Who is this who made her stop for a moment and pale? Her soul cries for mercy saying, *'Shahab, take me away from here.'* This roaring passion of love is expressed through his eyes ensures her to trust him, *' Yes Nargis, I will not let this candle melt in these infamous gatherings. I will come soon to take you away from this hell.'*

Shot 2- crane shot, a horse cart is coming on a lonely road. Shahab sits inside. The horse cart stops below down the balcony of the mansion of Nargis where she is waiting for him. She steps down from her balcony to meet him and both of them return back in the horse cart.

Monologue continues- At last the promised night ,for which Nargis has spent many uncomfortable nights standing on the windows of her dreams, has arrived.

Shot 3- Nargis is lying in the arms of Shahab.

Shahab: 'Nargis….Najjo , say something.'

Nargis: 'Shahab, are you really there?'

Shahab: 'Of course Najjo.'

Nargis: ' and I am there with you?'

Shahab: 'Yes Najjo. You are with me.'

Nargis: 'and you are taking me to your home? Your house is on a hill and is perfect white and I am wearing red wedding dress, getting down from the closed litter to step in the verandah of your house.'

The cart stops and Shahab and Nargis get down from the horse cart in front of his palatial house.

Scene No.: 2

Name of the scene: Reprimand scene

Time: Night

Location; Palatial House of Jalaluddine.

Shot 1: Shahab's father Jalaluddine stands with his family. His younger son Salim runs towards Shahab but is stopped by Jalaluddine.

Salim: 'Chacha jani...chacha jani.'

Jalal: 'stop'

Shot 2: Shahab and Nargis are scared . Jala moves towards them. They step back a little. Jalal chides him .

Jalal: 'How did you dare to marry and bring a prostitute to this house?'

Shahab: 'Baba, you cannot use such undignified words for her. She is my love and now is the daughter in law of this family.'

Jalal: 'Shut up, you cannot give this common abuse to my family. She is not our daughter in law but she is your crime.'

Hearing Jalal's acrimonious words Nargis runs out with her ears closed. Shahab stands stunned. Nargis stops the returning Horse cart.

Nargis: 'Allah: The cart wait... Wait.'

The cart man: 'where will you go, Bibiji;.'

Nargis: 'Take me to some cremation ground.'

She gets in to it to be lost in the dark.

Scene No.: 3

Name of the scene: Nargis leaving the Palace.

Time : Night

Location: Cremation ground

 Shot 1: 'The cart stops at the entrance of the cremation ground. Nargis gets down and asks the cart to return. The cart turns to return and Nargis looks at it moving away.

Monologue: 'Poor Nargis now stands alone in the terrible forest. Her wishes and dreams too are leaving her helpless.'

There cannot be a better introduction of a story , screen play , a film or a character than this one. Dancing on the beats of a classical 'Thumri' Nargis, the main female protagonist, hypnotizes her audience in the hall hiding a tempest within. The introduction reflects her background, profession and her emotional state. She is never tired of waiting for her love Shahab. When her wait comes to an end and Shahab actually arrives to take her, she is not able to believe her senses. She continues to feel as if it is still a dream that's why in his arms she wants to ensure by repeating her questions that it is indeed he and she is in her arms going to his home. . When she is convinced that Shahab is taking her to his home , she get another shock when she is insulted and humiliated by his father Jalaluddine who denies her an identity. Nargis who left her profession for a dignified life, is almost dead on this insult therefore what a better place could be for a dead than the cremation ground so she leaves to die a living death. Ordinarily this could only be an end but this is the beginning of the tale of Nargis. This leaves the audience struggling till end to find a culmination of the suspense of the story.

The introduction of Nargis in the monologues creates sympathy of the audience for her from the beginning and gets their endorsement of the relationship between Nargis and Shahab. When Jalal refuses to accept her and calls her a prostitute instead of his daughter in law , her dreams are shattered. This shock is no less painful for the audience as it is for Nargis herself. While this pain and sympathy for Nargis makes her a martyr, the rejection of her love by Jalal creates an anger for him. Her trauma brings her close to her audience from where her story moves forward.

A mix of commentary and the dialogues is a unique experiment in communication. With so much of variation in the story and the screen play one is floored by an extraordinary beginning of the film. This gives impetus to the film for more sensitive and emotional entertainment which continues till the end.. The time of the event i.e. the night combined with effects of horse hoofing and cart moving, chiming of ankle bells on the Thumri music and the location that creates an unenviable ambience of a red light area with oral commentary introducing the character escalates the interest in the introduction itself. The imaginative choice of place of event, location and the cremation ground is an example of innovative ideas.

2. The complications : The cause , action and relationship are used logically to create complications, conflicts and the tension in the story otherwise the story will be a poor narrative without twists and turns that will not interest anyone. The complications and conflicts appearing one after another immediately after the resolution of a problem are necessary to build up interest and subsequent release of tensions till another complication appears. This provides relief to the audience after intense situations are resolved.

Complications can be long and short but they should have appropriate relevance and reasons. If there is proper coordination and linkage between them the story will move forward without interruptions in its continuity and they will complement each other in the progression of the plot. If exclusion of any of them does not make a difference to the narration then such complications will not be acceptable.

3. **Contradiction, confrontation and relief:** This should take about 2/3 of the total time of the film which includes different ups and downs, tensions, confrontation and opposition etc. It is like ECG graph where modulations go up and down then there are straight lines before modulations go up again. This forms a major portion of the film or television story where characters play their established roles and help built up the conflicts and release of tension. Special attention is to be paid to develop this part which is also called *'the middle'*. It requires a great deal of vision and creativity. While doing so *'cause and effect'* should be used with logic and precision. A scene without a logic and reasonability destroys its dramatic effect. Similarly the unbelievable complications which cannot be easily understood by people should be avoided as they will not impress people and leave them confused.

Romance plays a very interesting role in screenplay or

television drama. It has an inherent emotion of everybody's life. Their internal and mostly suppressed feelings are awakened when they see another couple romancing on the screen. It is not necessary that every romance has a similar angle. As we have seen in the list of 37 plots there are only few of them which have romantic connotations however 'Romance' should always be integrated in the plot as it has the potential to have people glued to the screen.

4.The final solution- This part of the story takes the audience to its logical conclusion which includes its climax. There is no formula to have a set resolution of the problem. It largely depends on the sensitivity of the story, type of audience ,the personal preference of the director and the writers who decide how to approach a resolution whether it should be tragic or a happy one. While deciding so the basic nature and the emotional factor of the story should not be ignored otherwise the impact of the climax will be diluted and the audience will leave the theatre unsatisfied. There is a general tendency of those who see films only for entertainment to appreciate a happy end of the film however director is not bound to accept it.

Selection of characters:

It is next important task for a director after he is aware of commonly used characters and the locations as enumerated by Wycliffe. According to Wycliffe there can be a protagonist, an antagonist and the female lead character from the list. Thereafter few or more locations as required in the script can be selected where most of the events of the story occur.

Now any one of the 37 basic plots mentioned above can be

chosen for a plot to develop a story. There are only three objectives of a protagonist to accomplish-

1.To acquire an authority, possession or ownership

2.To get rid of something,

3. Revenge

These three points can be explained and analyzed as under-

A. Authority or ownership: 1.Vehicleor an aircraft or a ship, 2.Means of luxury, 3.Family, 4.Children, 5.Kids,6.Clothes, 7.ornaments and jewelry, 8. Immovable Property, 9.Other's possessions, 10.Popularity, 11.Formula, 12.Wealth, 13.social status and Dignity, 14.Knoledge, 15.Inheritance, 16.Love, 17.Map, 18.Fortune, 19.Pet animals, 20.Authority and the post, 21, independent Identity.

B. Getting rid off or revenge: 1.Law breaker, 2.Critic, 3.Killer, 4.Insult, 5.tyrant, 6. Enemy, 7.Advocate, 8.Opponent, 9.Decoit, 10.Desreputer, 11.Rumour monger, 12.Dictator,

Road blocks:

To accomplish his objectives the protagonist generally faces the following road blocks or the hurdles-

1. Facing a person who is more experienced, powerful, knowledgeable, wealthy, influential, beautiful or balanced than him.

2. Poverty, filth, domestic, incompetent, foolish, sick, lazy, latecomers, weak, stranger, Misinformation, mistaken identity of a person, Place and Object, Identity marks, Bloodstains,

Disable, ugly, criminal, Blind, Deaf, Dumb.

3. Suspicious, Convict, Infamous, Mental, Loss of memory, Misunderstanding/misunderstood, Hate, Loathsome, Unwelcome.

4. Gutless, Power, Friend, Influence, Dignity, Freedom, Closeness, Defensiveness, crime, Investigation, Extradited.

5. Opposition from an enemy, competitor, tyrant, executer of a punishment, punishment, Voice of conscience, Ego, Pride, Conventions, Rituals.

6. Duty bound, Commitment, Traditions, Religion, Status, Vow, Rules and regulations, Legalities, Laws, to save a friend or close relatives. 7. Disabled by extra baggage, Lack of identity, Truthfulness, Honesty, Dead end to prove ones merits.

The hero has to face and overcome these hurdles to achieve his ambitions and hit the targets. They can be accomplished by Begging, sacrifice or confrontation to win the targets.

A. Begging-The protagonist begs the giver to hand over his desired object. In most of the cases his request is accepted. Following can be the reasons for prayers/request or begging-

1. A right opportunity, another opportunity, Mercy.

2. Selling oneself at a cost, Duty, Devotion, service, Misunderstandings, Innocence, Fair intentions.

3. To honor a commitment, Vow, , to prove innocence, to save/defend others.

4. Defensive actions against an opponent to save a friend or

relative or love from harm.

5. Crime instigated by other, Misguidance about an identity, Revenge for a friend, relative or love.

B. Sacrifice-In the eventuality of a sacrifice there is a compromise between two opposing groups where both of them sacrifice something for other with certain conditions. This can also be termed as 'Compromise on mutual consent. Once this compromise is reached both the groups/parties are bound to honor the commitment made in the compromise terms and conditions. Normally following materials are sacrificed in a compromise-

1. Life, Love, Dignity, Health, Relation, freedom for self or loved ones.

2. Trust, Pleasure, Status, Valuable possessions, Friendship, respect for self or loved ones.

3. Self respect, Duty, Honor, Dignity, Vows and commitments, Time, Soul, Post, Money or property, Defensive actions.

4. Right to revenge and wining.

5. Pleasures and materials, essentials of life, important information or mystery, Getting rid of unpleasant situations of a friend, relative or loved ones.

C. Hitting the target- In the efforts to win and achieve its objective both the parties try their best of muscle power and physical strength, mental and spiritual powers and convince each other to give up their obstinacy. These persuasive powers can be in the following forms-

1. Arguments, threat, physical conflict.

2. Right to conquer and hitting the targets.

3. Stop further progression, Capsize, Sudden attack or loss to enemy, misinformation, revenge, convince him to change his mind and attitude by physical strength or talks., Disarming of fighting weapons, Injuring or killing the enemy,

4. Physical and mental dismemberment of the opponent or forcing surrender.

It is not a child's play to write a story but a writer can follow the conventional methods of selection of characters, places, events and integrate them logically with the convincing cause of action related to reasons, actions and relations. One should remember that any story starts with an Idea which is developed with great efforts and application of knowledge, language and technical skills. The story develops gradually step by step to its culmination. There s a regular chain of events when an idea takes off to its expansion till its climax. There are few common climaxes or end for a story such as-

1. A sick, disabled or a lost person appears suddenly.
2. The victory of the antagonist converts to his defeat and destroys him or there is a sudden victory of the Hero who almost lost his battle.
3. The crime was just a misunderstanding.
4. The character is either identified wrongly or he appears to be in disguise.
5. Unexpected sacrifice by unexpected characters.
6. There is a windfall for the person who sacrificed everything.

1. Acceptance of guilt by the antagonist or his surrender in the end.
2. The person gets a life that lost all hopes to live.
3. Submission of a evidence by a small character that decides the guilt and the defeat or punishment of the antagonist.
4. Sudden Change or reversal of situations between the protagonist and the antagonist.
5. Sudden appearance of some evidences that proves the truthfulness of the character and removes misunderstandings.
6. A miracle that reverses the entire scenario of disappointment to a pleasant surprise.

According to Wycliffe there cannot be any plot formation beyond these contents. Imagination can create an entertaining and interesting story out of any of the above suggestions. There can be **'experimental plots'** which can defy the set formula of storytelling and the contents. It depends on the writers or director's innovative thinking and creative imagination.

Wycliffe never promises to make anyone a story writer but only guide him. Every writer has its own style which is embellished by practice during the course of time therefore it is suggested to all the writers to read as much as they can to acquire knowledge about writing styles of different writers of different genres and work out his own unique style of story writing.

XXXXX

Scene 7:
The Screen play

The plot as we all understand in a layman's language that is a piece of land which is uneven, undeveloped with lot of shrubs and unproductive grass, trees and plants etc. This plot needs to be worked upon from its leveling to prepare a concrete plan of construction. Similarly in the plot of a story whether it originates from an idea, concept ,a short story, a novel or any other work of writing, there comes a series of changes and modifications by the time the screenplay reaches to its culmination. Most of these changes are carried out to sustain interest and an easy grasp to the audience. The common thread to these modifications is the continuity and integration of various facets of the story which restricts the diversion of the main content. This forms the *'theme'* of the story.

The way a written play is the base of a 'Drama' before it is staged, screenplay is the basic requirement for a film before it is shot. The screenplay in fact, is a detailed creative written impression of the film that is envisaged to be seen on the screen. In simple words one can say a screenplay is a film on paper which contains a detailed visualization however its outcome depends on its effective execution . It can easily be surmised that *written words* in a story or a Novel are not complete expression in a stage play or a screen play. They are complete only with the integration and incorporation of various genres of art forms and the technology. In the novels or the stories, written words are complete creative expression of a writer. There is no need of any other tools, means or technology to complement his creative expressions other than the words. Words are the only bridge required between a writer and the reader but is not so in the production of a play or a film where words are only a means to take off the flight of imagination to write a drama or a screenplay.

The imagination poured in the screenplay can be realized only with the support of sensitive performances of actors, effective dialogue delivery, attractive set design and the setting, special lighting, soulful background music etc beside eye catching cinematography and flawless editing .In their absence the film will neither be complete nor effective. Therefore it is confirmed that a screenplay is not complete in itself and it is the plinth for planning structure of a dramatic enactment or a film production. There is always scope for improvements at various stages of production.

Fundamentally film making is a director's medium that's why he is called *'the captain of the ship'* so the director must never lose control over the development of screen play while it is conceived by a writer. It is more important when the screenplay is not written by the director himself and he takes support of one or more writers in the process. If writers have functional knowledge of cinema techniques, it becomes easier for a director and writers to understand and coordinate with each other otherwise there may be occasional conflicts between them. Writers depend more on *'Dialogues'* than the visualization while director is more concerned about *visuals*. In such an eventuality the director must use his authority and convey what exactly he thinks about certain things.

The selection of an original story provides more freedom to the director and the writer to mould its presentation than an adapted literary work or a novel where the author has already worked out details extensively however there is always a gap between the concepts of a writer and the film director. In case of adaptations the writer normally is not on the same page as that of the director who would like to take some cinematic liberties to revise already written work to suit the cinematographic presentation and the commercial viability. This happens due to lack of knowledge of the author about cinema ,technical requirements and economics of cinema. It is a great dampener for a director to accept a renowned or a published literary work as it is.

When a director decides to work on such adaptations he should be more careful, decisive and sensitive towards the basic sentiments of the story to avoid hurting the writer . In such cases the director must take the author in to confidence about the impending changes or modifications in the story before he intends to start work on the subject. This will save lot of their time in unproductive engagements and also reduce, if not completely avoid, the conflicts and confrontations between them. The director must understand that as the film is so dear to him , the story is similarly close to the heart of the author however if working together, both the author and the director must respect and accommodate each other. They should not be adamant to plough the field as per their whims.

The mind as we all know never stands still even in sleep and so is the vision of a director when he is engaged in film writing. He is constantly on his thinking mode at any point of time. New ideas emerge and vanish with time. Some are useful and some are better forgotten. In such cases director must keep a note of every idea that strikes him related to the performance of the actors, special set design or setting, camera angles etc. This continuous flow of ideas and their notes help director to be more precise and clear in his concept.

The director should remember the following guidelines while writing a screenplay:

1. He should make notes of minute details and the ideas in every scene. It is not necessary that his opinions may be part of the draft script but should be included in the final version of the draft so that everybody knows about them.

2. A screenplay should be clearly written and attractively bound for the presentation to the financiers, actors, distributors and other relevant people. This script is a trailer of the final film.

3. A detailed screenplay helps understand the sentiments and emotions of different characters.

If the director does not prepare the notes of his imaginative ideas and innovative thoughts, that keep on hitting him, it is possible that he may forget when he needs them most. This may force him to compromise with the concept or he may prefer to shoot the story in its original form. Both these situations are detrimental and the director would not remain the sole creator of its original work but be labeled as a mere translator of the original work of the author. In another likely situation if the writer lacks the knowledge of cinematic language, he would overload the screenplay with *dialogues* and miss out the visualization of scenes thus reducing the impact of inherent emotions and sentiments. The writers should know that film is a visual medium and should understand the intricacies of its presentation.

The extensive technical details about a scene are best be avoided or reduced to minimum if their mention is indeed important, such as camera angles, special sound effects, specific expressions required in actors' performances may find a place in the scene to enhance the reading effect. '*Actions*' of the actors and camera angles and movements may be specified before shooting. It is not appropriate to decide the '*action*' as per the shots but shots should be divided as per the action required in the screenplay. It is also true that after a long experience only a director is able to form a clear visual concept but still he should make extra efforts to visualize the scenes beforehand. It makes it easy to visualize the final form of the film.

Screen play writing- The journey:

The journey to write a screenplay begins with an idea, short story, Novel or an adaptation of a literary work. They are only take off points from where the screenplay makes its first move forward. If the director himself writes the screenplay it becomes easier for him to develop it in the manners he conceives the film but it is not always possible. A director may have to work with one or more regular or temporary writers engaged by the studio or a production house. If the film is based on a literary work the director has to deal with the author and write the script respecting his sentiments. It is also possible that the story is a pure fantasy of the author. In this case the director is mostly dependent on the writer and his contribution in the form and style is negligible. It is a pathetic situation for a creative director. In different situations director has to make special efforts to co-operate, co ordinate and accommodate other's opinions and discover his own style and functional methodology in the process. It is ultimately the director's responsibility to present an attractive, innovative, imaginative and creative script to his financiers, distributers and the lead actors. An experienced director can accomplish the same with his original ideas or the salient features of the story presented without a proper and detailed script. To do it the director needs to have a clear vision about the film which reflects his own creative style and identity. Based on this preliminary concept the director may write a synopsis of the screenplay that has précised narration of the main story. If he is successful to convince financiers, producers, distributors and the main actors he can proceed to write a detailed screenplay along with other writers. While writing the scenes writers and director should integrate necessary emotional, effective and technical details to continue refreshing and refurbishing the concept of the film in their mind.

Screen time:

An entire gamut of events taking place in the story may take more than few decades in real time which is contracted within two to three hours of screen time. It may be done in such a way that audience doesn't feel the distortion in real time. While doing so unnecessary events are deleted and only those are kept which have some bearing and relevance to develop important characters and take the story forward. Care should be taken to ensure that all the characters, events and the scenes are emotionally, aesthetically and physically integrated and have logical relationship and continuity with the plot, inherent sentiments and proper timing. The timing can be reduced or increased as required in the scene for example action scene have to be faster than the emotional ones but every scene has to be developed in such a way that every event has an illusion to be happening in real time. There is no mathematical calculation to determine the duration of each scene. It depends on the director's vision and requirement of the story.

Time lapse:

The most important factor in managing time is *'time lapse'* that takes place between the transitions from one scene to another. The time lapse can be indicated by various means like a 'dissolve' in which a scene fades out and another appears simultaneously. **Dissolve** is the most popular device that is understood easily by the audience. Day and night scenes can be easily identified so there is no need for any direct indication or special effect.

It is not necessary that time lapse should always be indicated if not required, by a clock or a calendar as most of the times audience can make out time lapse taking place in the flow of the story. Another popular method to inform about the time lapse is through Dialogues where characters give an indication about the time and the place following transition to the next scene. Similarly when the transition time is short, this can be shown by direct entry and exit movements from one place to another.

Parallel action:

Other devices to manage time include *parallel actions* in different scenes taking place simultaneously in different locations. This method is considered to be more entertaining and interesting ,it is used to increase tension and curiosity.

There is more scope for managing screen time in this method as for example; two different actions in different locations may appear on screen for about two minutes but in reality that action might take more than ten minutes. So in parallel scenes contraction and extension of screen time can be done more conveniently and smoothly without disturbing the sense of real time. This authenticates the saying that *'a film is not a reality but a feeling of realism'.*

Most of the management of screen time is accomplished by director and the editor when the film is on the editing table however it is important to take shots of similar action from various angles to provide choice of cutting and maintain continuity. This saves lot of screen time of a particular action.

Similarly by extending the length of the shots screen time of an action can be extended if required in the scene. If an action is shot without cuts it will have the duration of real time but if the same is divided in many shots, the editor can save lot of screen time by cutting unnecessary action, pauses and gaps to reduce the length of the scene.

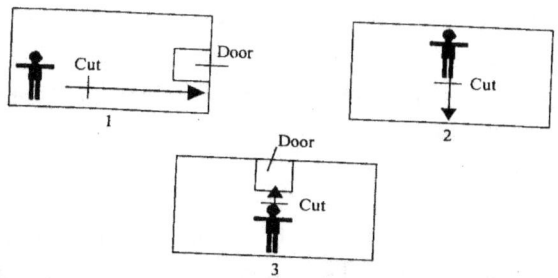

1.Takes from various angles.

The originality of the story is not as important as its honest expression. Since film production is for public consumption there has to be an effort to ensure a continuous flow of emotions and sentiments of the characters in an unified manners to keep the audience glued to the screen till the end of the film. This helps audience to become part of the story and they start identifying them as the characters on screen. A success here is the success of the film and its director. Therefore the director should present its characters and various emotional situations in such a way that people identify with them and have the same sentimental feeling.

Every director has his own unique style to conceive a story and his characters which is generally influenced by his own upbringing, knowledge and experiences. Every film claims to be complete in itself but if the audience don't show there interest in it, these claims appear hollow.

Characterization:

Every character in the story has a distinct personality, identity and emotions that is designed and developed by a writer and a director in their own styles. If the story is based on human relationship the director should first start visualizing his various characters and follow it to decide their behavioral patterns to look the characters normal so that they identify with people as one among them. This is done with director's own or acquired experiences.

The process of characterization is one of the most important factors in film making where director must fully convince himself about their authenticity to convince his audience later. That's why it is more important for a director to prepare a mental sketch about his characters before he starts writing the screenplay. A new director may consult other experienced people in this task. An astute director who observes various characters around him in day to day life is benefitted in long run to acquire sufficient knowledge and experience about their behavior, their living and their attitudes etc. *'Observation'* is as important for actors as it is for a director who are benefitted by their minute behavior and mannerism. The knowledge acquired by actors reflects in their performance.

Flexibility:

It is always advisable that director steps in to shooting floor with his imaginative film written with complete plan on paper. This provides him confidence and clarity on the set. It does not mean that the director must be so rigid about his plan that he cannot change a bit of it to include suggestions given by others. Once complete planning is done and a functional screen play is finalized, it is normal for a director to proceed with shot division however his cameraman may like to modify the shot division and the actors may come out with their suggestions on their performance. Keeping these suggestions in mind their can always be some changes or modifications in the script, which director should not resist and consider them with an open heart. His rigidity may shut the doors for further interaction with his creative team members who may avoid to air their opinions frankly even if they are for better. Most of these suggestions come during the rehearsals where there is ample scope for improvement so they should never be restricted but appreciated by the director. This flexibility creates a better understanding and pleasant working atmosphere within the unit members.

The scenario: A scenario is defined as :

'The outline or the manuscript of a motion picture or television program, underlining the actions, the description of scenes and characters etc. in the order in which they take place.'

No director prefers a screen play where shot divisions or minute details of the scene are predetermined where he has to forgo his creative freedom and own contribution therefore the director is always prepared to accommodate any opinion and suggestion for changes coming from anybody. It does not mean that director starts shooting without a scenario. Shot division of the scene is done as per the visualization of an action and is normally done on the set prior to the shooting in the presence and consultation with his cameraman and the actors. The shot division is required to facilitate the editor to reconstruct the scene in a continuous action. The advantage of having a scenario allows a director to peep in to the minute emotions of the characters and modify them if required before the shoot. It also guides the crew members to take technical decisions accordingly.

Normally there are two types of directors, first one are those who write each and every minute detail in the script before the shoots and others are those who have the mental sketch of every scene ready in their mind, rest of the decisions like shot division, camera placement, movements and angles, setting etc are taken on the set itself. I Keep myself in the second category where the script is only a means to remind you of the continuity of the scenes. My grasp on the story of the film and its every scene, development of characters and their emotions, creating an ambience for the scene etc inspires me .It boosts my creative energy and gives me confidence about the final result that would be better than my original vision. While writing the screenplay director should also involve the editor to make him understand about the rhythm of the film. It will avoid complications during editing process. If not, Editor may then have to resort to the use of cutaways and close ups to maintain the required pace.

A screenplay must be '**Homogeneous**' and '**Precise**'. The director must do his home work properly to ensure how he would shoot a scene. He may have extensive discussions with his crew members for a clear vision about their functional strategy, technical requirements, emotional effect and their expectations from him to avoid confusions at any level. While shooting director must behave like a leader and a guide to his unit members and not become their follower. An inexperienced director should hone his directorial skills instead of depending on others.

Dialogues:

Dialogues are an important tool for the characters to communicate and express their emotions, opinions and philosophy in film and television fictions. The dialogues give a distinct identity to every character differentiating their style of delivery. In a stage performance the dialogues have to be heard by the last man sitting in the extreme corner of the theatre therefore they have to speak them aloud in high pitch and volume . Due to technological advancements in cinema and television the characters speak with their natural emotions. One can say that in theatre the dialogue are forced to hear but in cinema they are spoken normally. In cinema camera captures the minutest expressions on the face of an actor by placing it at various angles and distances from close shot to the long shots therefore the dialogues are spoken as per the emotional requirement of the character. While watching a play audience have to be sitting in fixed position, at the fixed distance and angle from the stage so the dialogues are delivered in different style in both these medium. The dialogues must complement inherent emotions and the expressions of the scene and should avoid unnecessary details. Similarly the language of dialogues should not be too literary and tough to understand but should be simple and communicative. It sometimes can be touchy to make audience feel the similar emotions as that of the characters. Actors may be permitted to do minor alterations in the dialogues to suit their performance. Many times it happens that the actor in a comedy or an actions scene may prefer to write his own dialogues to complement his unique style. Where there is a need to provide more information the use of background commentary or narration may be useful. Writer should avoid writing lengthy and long winding dialogues but write short and to the point. The lengthy dialogues if required may be interrupted by aural reactions to break the monotony of the scene.

Example: **Film: Devdas**

Scene No...,   Location: Chandramukhi's house

Time: Day Characters: Devdas, Chandramukhi.

1. **Devdas lies on his bed with empty bottles of alcohol and glasses scattered around. Chandramukhi looks at him. Devdas pours liquor from the bottle in to his glass and throws the bottle away. Chandramukhi comes to him and he hangs down in hangover.**
   Chandramukhi: 'Don't drink more Devdas...'
   Devdas: 'Why?'
   Chandramukhi: 'You started drinking since few days. You will not be able to tolerate this much'.
   Devdas: 'who the bastered is who drinks to tolerate'. I drink to breath. I have no strength to move out from this place that's why I am lying here and keep looking at you even then I don't lose my senses. Some consciousness is always left. Tell my senses that I should never be in senses.

2. **Devdas comes near to Chandramukhi.**
   Chandramukhi: 'There are people coming here who don't ever touch the liqueur.'
   Dev stumbles. Chandramukhi lends her support to him. He sits down.
   Dev: 'They don't even touch it...? If I have a gun I will shoot them. They are greater evil than me chandramukhi. First I will not leave drinking and if at all I leave it then I will never return back to this place. I have a cure but what about them who don't drink and still come here. **(Chandramukhi tries to hold him)**

Don't touch me chandramukhi, I still have some senses left.

Devdas gets up and throws the glass on the floor. Glass pieces scatter around

Devdas: ' You don't know how much I hate you people and will continue to hate them but still I will keep on coming here , sit beside you and talk to you. What else is the remedy but can you understand it? People commit sins in the dark and drink here in the light.'

This scene is one of the best examples of not only dialogue writing but also of a fine delivery. The simplicity of the language and the short length of dialogues straight away hits your emotions. Therefore dialogues should never be stretched beyond the acceptable limits.

Inspiration and adaptation:

Many film makers believe that the success of a film can be ensured if it is based on a successful play, Novel or inspired from an earlier successful film. It is true that originality of the work is not necessary either for making or the success of a film. Story can be adapted or inspired from any event, individual, literary work, Novel, play or a film made earlier. It is called *'Adaptation'*. Those directors who don't want to take a risk with an original story prefer to go for an adaptation hoping for a sure success but it is not so.

Adaptation- Novel:

When a story is adapted from a novel or a play the screen

writer should try to visualize the film with least deviation from the original vision and concept of the original author however creative liberties can be availed for the medium taking the author in to confidence. This helps to establish a better understanding and coordination between the author and the film writer and director. Adaptation of other's work also requires a great deal of imagination and creative merits of screen play writer. Generally a novel reading cannot be accomplished in one sitting therefore writing of a novel or other literary work is dominated by **'words'** where every written word has its own effect and influence on the reader while a film which is watched in one sitting from beginning to end, is expressed by its **'visuals'**. The visuals have more impact than written words so any adaptation should predominantly consist of *'visualization'* without hurting the sentiments of the original imagination of the author within the screen time restrictions for a film.

It is always not true that every adaptation can lead to a successful film. If it would be so then every adaptation could rake mullahs for its producer and no film could be made on a original story. The success of any creative work that includes a play, novel or any other form depends on many factors such as period, socio economic situation, atmosphere and culture and above all the generation of people therefore it is not necessary that if something was successful earlier will be so even today. Similar is the case with remakes of earlier successful films . All remakes may not be so appealing and convincing. This can be proved by the success and failure of many films based on the Novel *'Devdas'* of the same name authored by *Sharat Chandra* in the year 1907.The story reflected the social discrimination, economic deprivation, unacceptability of love marriages and social status of women who struggles to find her place in the society. The first film in 'Devdas' series was made in the year 1935 which was highly successful as people could identify with the content and its characters. After Indian independence another film with the similar name was produced by Octogenarian film maker *Bimal Roy* in the year 1952 with Dilip Kumar as Devdas. Dilip Kumar has re-lived the same magic with his histrionic performance. It is said that this is the best film of over a dozen films made on the novel till date. The recent film 'Devdas' made with an astronomical budget with shahrukh Khan in the main lead failed to entice people due to its poor casting and characterization, distortion of period, socio economic situation of the characters and an attempt to modernize the content that altered the basic sentiments and emotions of the story. It made the film a cocktail that could neither become a modern tale nor preserved its original vision. The film was a great disappointment for the cinegoers. Therefore one should never make an effort for whatever creative or professional reasons to distort the original thoughts and concept of the author when ever such adaptations are made in to a film. Any deviation or distortion in its period and socio economic conditions of the characters that have permanent imprints in the memory challenges the audience's knowledge, intelligence and thoughts which is normally not appreciated. Creative modifications in the work should be carried out within the limits of the original vision and sensitivities.

The enormous challenge is faced by a screen play writer when he works on an adaptation of a literary form that is more *'verbose'* . It cannot be effectively communicated in a film form. This *verbal form* has to be transformed in to *visual form* in which a shot says many things that takes one or more paragraphs in a novel. This cannot be done by reducing dialogues but the entire verbal scene has to be recreated in visual form with special attention given to maintain *'filmic time'*. Adaptation of a written form in to visual form is an extensive exercise where every scene from the beginning to end is recreated generally to the dislike of the original author.

The basic difference between a novel and the play can be explained by their structure. A novel expresses an opinion with more creative and imaginative freedom in which author's unrestricted imagination allows him unlimited opportunities to develop his characters, situations and emotions more extensively than a play where the characters are restricted to display their emotions in limited actions in a limited space of a stage thus reducing the scope of expressions and performance.

In the adaptation of a novel there is a problem of selection of the story and contracting its content to the limited screen time. In a play adaptation does not only requires a complete visual restructuring of scenes but also needs to introduce new characters and new situations . It cannot be restricted to the vision and space of a theatrical production. The success of a play largely depends on the performance of its actors and the sleekness of stage production, it is not possible and not required for a film like shouting of dialogues and moving fast on the stage for a loud acting.

Adaptation-Play:

If someone is inspired by a story or adapts a play for a film it is better for him to pick up the essence or the main idea of the story and conceive a screen play with an entirely new vision and concept instead of translating the play itself. A mere translation of the play will devoid the film of its basic elements of cinema and the film will just be a visual presentation of the play as captured by a camera. So, one should desist from literal translation of a play while writing a screen play as it would be a waste of time and money. It does not mean that a film cannot be made on the successful plays. A well known Marathi play *'Toh me navech'* was adopted for its successful Hindi film *'Woh main Nahin'* and recently another very successful film *'Aankhen'* and *'Oh my God'* were adaptations of renowned Gujrati plays however more care should be taken when adapting and visualizing a play for a film. Those play writers who decide to make film on their work themselves face a bumpy road ahead due to their lack of film sense and knowledge of technology which is essential for writing screen play.

Example: **Film- 'Ankhen'**

Scene No.. ..   **Time: Day**

Location: Bank

Characters: Rajput, Iliyas, Vishwas, Delnaaz, Prem, Sailesh, Arjun   and others.

People   step down on the stairs to gather in a hall. Arjun stands with his gun pointing at others. Iliyas also holds a gun. People are scared. The bank is being robbed. Vishwas stops someone running away breaking the alarm circuit to close the doors. Delnaaz and Prem too join him. Sailesh tries to abscond when Arjun and Vishwas fire at him.

Rajput: Don't fire please don't fire.

Vishwas: 'Number one, kill everyone.

Iliyas: 'Yes, if anyone dares to move I will take out his eyeballs and her too.'

Vishwas: 'will you...?'

Delnaaz: 'who... me...?'

Vishwas: 'Yes, you.. You do it. I will count up to ten. You go down and return with the jeweler box. Keep that on this red handkerchief.

Delnaaz: Please count up to twenty. The box is very heavy.'

Rajput: 'Do as I say. Hurry up.'

Prem: 'Sir, If Delnaaz says it is heavy it must be true."

Viswas: 'Then you to go with her . one...tw...thre...fore.. five.. six....'

Rajput: Sailesh, what are you doing. Don't run in front of enquiry counters.'
Sailesh comes to Iliyas and points his gun to his mouth. Vishwas and Arjun too point their gun at him.

Sailesh: 'a...a...a...'

Vishwas: ' No one will move. We have told you .'

Sailesh: 'sorry... sorry.'

Iliyas: 'Do you think yourself too wise...?'

Sailesh: Sorry. It is done by mistake.'

Iliyas: 'Ok, what were you doing herebastered?'

Sailesh: I was going to check the vehicle.'

Iliyas: 'Vehicle... do I clear the waist from your carburetor?'

Sailesh: 'I am the only son of my father.'

Iliyas: 'What? Do you have only one father.? Tell me.'

Sailesh: ' Only one mother and only one father.'

Iliyas: ' only one father and one mother. Behaving wise to me. Come open your mouth.'

Sailesh: 'a...a...'.

Iliyas: 'open your mouth.'

Sailesh: 'aaa.aaa.'

Iliyas: ' Yes, now keep it in your mouth like a tooth brush. (The gun drops out of his mouth but Iliyas could not see it. He hears Sailesh and looks at the gun. Now what has dropped down.. what is it. He tells Sailesh to put the gun in his mouth again.)

Sailesh: ' Gun.'

Iliyas asks him to open his mouth threatening.

Iliyas: 'Pick it up and put it back in to the mouth.'

Sailesh : 'Open your mouth.'

159

Iliyas: ' oh keep it in your mouth and not mine. (Sailesh keep the gun in to his mouth)Correct. Now keep standing here like this. People are looking at you and your new tooth brush.'Veiko vajradanti.'

Vishwas counts: 'Fourteen...fifteen...sixteen..seventeen..

Delnaaz and Prem return back with the jeweler box. Vishwas and Iliyas move Rajput and Sailesh at gun point. Vishwas pushes Rajput and the trio closes the shutter. Rajput and others come to the shutter. Keep it there on the red cloth.

Rajput begs him: 'see this is our customers' jeweler. Please don't take it.'

Vishwas: 'Number three. Take this box and go out.'

Rajput: 'See. Listen to me. You cannot sell this jewelry in the market.'

Vishwas: ' You shut up and keep quiet.'

Rajput: 'Please accept what I say.'

Iliyas: You shut up.'

Rajput: 'we can sit to gather and negotiate quietly.'

Vishwas :' You will not say anything.'

Rajput : we can talk.... Talk reasonably...we can. Please listen to me...You can't...'

Vishwas: 'I say you shut your mouth.'

Rajput: 'You are committing a crime. This jewelry...'

Vishwas shouts: 'shut up.'

Rajput: ' where are you taking it/ see. Just look at me.'

Vishwas: Number three...'

Rajput: 'See, you can't escape. I am telling you please...'

Vishwas: Number one....'

Rajput: 'yes... yes...'

Iliyas: ok...ok...'

Vishwas: 'are you ready...?'

Rajput: Yes...

Iliyas: yaa...uuu...'

Rajput: oye...'

Vishwas: 'where is the car?'

Sailesh: 'It is there... there.' Vishwas, **Arjun and Iliyas get in to the jeep. There comes a security van. Iliyas tells the driver to take the vehicle to Byculla station.**

Iliyas: take the car to the Byculla station quickly.'

Arjun: 'Who is it....'

Vishwas :sit down first. I will tell you everything. Now do it and move.'(everyone looks at them from the other side of the shutter.)

Sailesh: 'Ok sir.'

Iliyas: 'are you blind. Do you drive the car with jerks?

Arjun: 'Ooh...'

Iliyas: 'Put the gear...'

The jeep runs on the road to Byculla.

The above mentioned scene is one of the excellent examples of the adaptation from a play in the film *'Aakhen'*. The plan to rob a bank by a trio of blind persons Arjun, Vishwas and Iliyas keeps the audience in tenterhooks till the end of the film. It keeps the curiosity alive in every passing frame. The plan to execute a bank robbery by a group of three blind men without letting anyone know of their blindness is not only inconceivable but also unbelievable. It is sufficient to keep their interest ever rising. People know that robbers are blind and this fact is intermittently brought to the fore by emphasizing their mistaken actions such as mouth opening by Sailesh and falling of the gun without being seen by Iliyas and others as a reminder of their disability. Similarly Vishwas and Arjun continue committing silly mistakes which are noticed by the audience but not by those present in the Bank. The confusion created by tiny mistakes of these blind men keep audience entangled with the robbery plan for which they are not sure that would really be successful.

Rajput is the main anchor who double crosses and pretends to be with the bank staff in their critical hours as well as coordinates bank robbery with the trio. He is motivated to execute it to take revenge with the Bank. He conceives a unique and foolproof plan to execute it with the help of blind people to keep everyone guessing. No one would ever think of a robbery by blind men who are his main accomplices. The film contains variety of actions to create curious moments throughout the film moving inch by inch to its climax. During the act of robbery the trio does not lose its originality and its normal behavior. Humorous dispositions of Iliyas help release some stressful moments. The struggle of bank officials to prevent this robbery and brutal confrontation of robbers create some really trying situations, helplessness and scare among bankers and the audience with their realistic performances. At no point of time it gives an impression except to the audience that the robbery is carried out by blind people and being coordinated by Rajput. The film in general and this scene in particular is a fine example of the dramatization of an action. The imaginative transformation to a dramatic action looks far more real than contrived one.

The knowledge of the outcome of a real action like a cricket , football match or a chase scene itself is enough to create curiosity as it is inherent in it which is not planned nor executed in a planned manner. The same is maintained in the film though the unbelievable act is planned but it looks real when executed. so people are unable to guess its outcome, similar to that of a police chasing a thief where nobody knows if the thief would be caught. With this logic it can be surmised that there are two types of action sequences one which are planned and other which are not therefore the writer must take care to see that an unplanned action scene does not look planned one or vice versa because the behavior of the characters in both the actions will be different and the outcome uncertain. This keeps the curiosity mounting till the end that leads to climax.

The documentary script:

It is bit uncomfortable to write screenplay for a documentary film. Everyone is aware that there is no story content in a documentary or a nonfiction film than how there could be a 'screenplay' therefore the format for a nonfiction is rightly nomenclature as *'Script'*. In journalistic jargons any written material is called a 'script' .

When *Lumiere Brothers* pioneered film making it was based on realistic content. In fact it was coverage of real events or reality as captured by camera without cuts that's why these films are known as *'single shot films'*. Subsequently the same style was extended to the coverage of news events which did not require a written script. In fact the word *'screenplay'* was not coined then and was unknown to anyone till the time. Those were the early years of experimentation in making films which gradually included individual imagination in the reality coverage. With the lapse of time and many innovations taking place in film technology, film makers also experimented with documentary on issues of social and national importance in addition to the coverage of news reels and reality films. In the initial years of cinema due to the absence of a written script the consumption of Raw film material was too high and expensive for shooting which not many could afford. Since there was no element of entertainment like its later incarnation of fiction films, it was difficult and it is still so to arrange money for making nonfiction films. Even then awakened film makers consider production of documentary films very important and challenging. The lack of money and enthusiasm of financiers in this field makes it more important that the director of a documentary works on his subject with in-depth research. Without in-depth study of the subject matter, the documentary will only be superficial and fail to impress its target audience.

In-depth research of the content related to the place, the personality, the issues and their resolutions makes a documentary maker more confident and sensitive about its success. While doing so the director is also informed about the local needs required for planning the shoots like availability of electrical power, transportation and local contacts that could be of immense help to him at the time of shooting.

Once the research is complete director with his imagination and the vision of the film proceeds with writing probable visuals and the supporting/corresponding words like dialogues, narration or commentary, tentative content of possible interviews and interaction with people related to the subject matter. A documentary script can only be accepted as a *'Guide line'* for the film that can be altered anytime before, during and after the shoots. A documentary script has generally more flexibility than its counterpart in fiction film. These are the advantages of working on draft script for a nonfiction film-

1. It provides clarity of purpose and concept of the subject matter.

2. It helps director to plan every visual and its corresponding sounds including commentary. If there is less to say in words the scene will be shorter and in contrast if there is more to say in the commentary the scene will be longer for which he will require to shoot more visual material with more number of

shots. Some scenes can also be planned which have music and the sound effects prominently.

3. The script works as a *'guide* 'to the film maker to remind him of every important scene and not to miss out any of them.

4. It brings   clarity about the content, specific *'time'* and *'Location'* of the shoots.

In the script for a documentary film there is nothing permanent or fixed that cannot be modified including visuals, sound and narration. That's the reason that a final version of a documentary may be completely different than what is conceived. These modifications during the production take place in the form of new information that keep on pouring and are included or something found redundant are deleted. It may so happen that something is not available /possible to shoot in a preconceived location or something may not be available at all which is managed with the use of still photographs or graphics and animation. Stock shots, paper clippings etc. Finally the commentary is rewritten complementing the visuals to include fresh information by a professional writer. This commentary and narration is different than that is written by the director himself in the draft script before shoots..

Documentary film: Khadi and Village Industries Commission

The film example from the documentary on *'Khadi and Village Industries Commission'* promotes the activities of the institution. Like advertisement films it does not promote a product but the dedication of KVIC to the cause of social service to the people of rural India. KVIC is an autonomous organization of the Indian government which was primarily established to realize the dreams of Mahatma Gandhi for the development and growth of rural society.

Scene 1:

1. L.S. Tilt down from sky to the courtyard of a house where many people are busy weaving cloth on looms.
2. M.C.S. two children fall on the heap of cloth.
3. C.U. The supervisor looks at them with anger.
   Supervisor- what have you done...scattered all the material.
4. As in shot 2. A lady the children's mother, lifts them up from the heap.
   Lady-- get up...get up.
5. C.U. The supervisor as in shot 3.
   Supervisor- why don't you take care of them?
6. M.C.S. Mother beats her children.
7. L.S. Trolley. A boy is reading some files on a table. A girl is doing something nearby. The boy gets up to set the children free.
   Girl- why are you beating them, Mamta ben?
   Boy- why don't you send them to school? Often I find them loitering here.
8. M.C.S. Mother and children
   Lady-- How do I send them to school? Their father does not pay their fee.
9. C.S. the boy convinces the lady.
   Boy- you should have told me earlier. You can do so. All the children of our institution staff study in 8th, 9th and 11th standard or they are in ITI. They also get scholarship under workers welfare scheme.

10. Some people listen to the boy standing nearby.

    Lady-I don't know anything about it.

11. C.S. the girl too starts talking-

    Girl- Now you know. Go and get your children admitted in school and I will try for their scholarship.

12. L.S. Men and women

13. .C.S. A lady removes thread from the loom.

Scene 2.

14. L.S.A senior officer is on the stage. A boy works on a spinning wheel.

15. M.C.S. some people stand near the stage.

16. C.S. Of a hand spinning on wheel.

17. C.S. of a hand pushing a button.

18. C.U. the light is on.

19. L.S. all the workers clap.

20. L.S.Tilt up.officer

    Officer-Brothers and sisters, you see a miracle on spindle wheel. You see, How fast it works. Now Khadi and village industries commission has manufactured a new type of spinning wheel. With this you can produce electricity while spinning. You can light up your home with this electricity.

21. L.S. Top angel. People clap.

22. L.S. A boy Madhav stands up on the stage.

    Madhav-Gandhi ji used to say, Khadi is a mission. Khadi is an employment of millions of unemployed people. It gives them to work with dignity. More over it pays them money and respect. Khadi gives them equal opportunity to grow and be equal.

23. M.L.S. People are clapping

'Khadi and Village Industries commission' is not an institution but an opportunity to underprivileged to learn new skills. It is involved in preserving the traditional past and innovating technology for the future. The innovative spinning wheel which also produces electricity to light up the darkness in the lives of rural folks, is an evidence of KVIC's passion for the poor.

Chronology of screen play:

Normally outline, synopsis, treatment and the screenplay are written in present tense as a film or a play is always seen or heard in the present except the *flash back* where story moves back ward to explain certain previous events   or moves to the future as character dreams or foresee things (*flash forward*) the way they would like to see it.. Even these flash backs and flash forwards are written in the present tense to facilitate easy understanding to the readers about the past or the future. Afterwards the reader returns back to the present and moves forward along with the story.

The subjective view point of the writer should be reflected in first person-plural as '*we*' and not as '*I*' for the reason that from the beginning itself the writer must give an impression to carry everybody along with him. This creates a sense of belonging among the members in the film unit with the subject. This may be remembered that everyone in the film unit is also a film viewer so if they develop an affinity and the interest in the subject, it also means that the film has established its relationship with the audience. There are few chronological steps to proceed with writing a screen play for a fiction film which a director and the writer must follow with due earnest however for some convenience and necessity any of the steps can be skipped or reworked till complete satisfaction is achieved. In all these stages the coordination and the understanding between the writer and the director is of utmost importance. They should be on the same plane.

1. **Synopsis:** This is the first step to write a complete synopsis of the story as to be seen in the film. The main advantage of synopsis is to facilitate the reaction from main actors, financiers, distributers and the producers. If they appreciate the synopsis the first successful step is taken forward. If the story is adapted from a novel or a play or an idea it may not be possible to narrate complete story in the same form in short time available for the purpose or it may not be grasped by others in the same spirit therefore a synopsis is the right form of narration that also depends on the style and effectiveness of the narrator. A synopsis does not require details of characters, situations, locations and development of the concept. This is written in the format of a short story where selected few characters and dramatic situations are developed in detail including the description of dialogues. It normally is not a complete play format nor is it a shooting script.

2. **Scenario:** In Scenario writers have to develop and visualize every scene to include visual description, characterization, probable actions and dialogues. In this stage scenes are discovered according to the requirement of the story that leads to the development of the screenplay thereafter. Scenario while clearing the mist of ideas, provides an opportunity to some enthusiastic writers and directors to display their imaginative and creative skills to understand the story themselves and explain the same to others.

3. **Functional outline or Treatment:** It is an extension of scenario in which every scene is described along with suggestions of dialogues and actors' performances. Many times writers combine the scenario and the treatment to save time and efforts.

4. Master scene script: The writers who are not a director themselves write complete dialogues along with brief description of the scene in the *Master scene script*. It is not necessary that whatever is written at this stage may be included in the final version of the screenplay however this is the last but not the least important stage of screenplay writing which plays an important role to conceive the *Blue print* and the Master scene script. The master scene script also helps producer and the director to work on the detailed production plan simultaneously while the final version of screen play is underway. In fact this is a '**Guide script'** before a final screenplay is attempted.

5. Screen play: By the time writer reaches to this stage, his vision about the scenes attains absolute clarity regarding the film's form before the actual shoots take off. This is the version which includes detailed visualization of scenes, probable action and dialogues. It is normally provided in bound form to the actors, cameraman and the art director and other crew members to visualize the entire film to work out their respective roles according to the director's vision in the screenplay. The screenplay also provides a window to the actors to peep in to their characters. Few directors may find this process of distributing the screen play copies to others redundant but they should not take it as a compulsion. They should accept it as a process to create understanding and clarity with his unit members and the technical team.

6. Shooting script: Before the shoots director's main task is to divide the scenes in shots. This process is called *'Shot division.'* Unlike the writing of the screen play from the first scene to the climax the shot division of the scenes in the shooting script is generally not undertaken in one go as it requires the details of the Shooting location/sets to decide possible camera and actors' movement for each shot which largely depends on the geography of the outdoor locations or the design of the sets. Therefore the shot division is taken up by the director in consultation with the cinematographer and the main actors before every shooting schedule when everything is finalized and director is sure of the locations and the set designs. Few directors take up shot division of the entire script and publish them in a book form for distribution among the crew members before shoots. This is practiced by many film makers abroad..

The shot division of a scene, from the film *'Toote Pankh'* directed by *Kuldeep Sinha* can be understood in the following example.

Scene 1.
Title: Back Home (as written in the script)
Location: A lonely rural pathway, exterior, Day- sunset.
Characters: Dayal, Cart rider

1.Sunset. A horse cart is moving forward on an isolated pathway of countryside. Dayal is sitting on the rear seat deeply drowned in his thoughts. Dayal returns home after many years.
Monologues: 'Such a transformation of this place in few years or nothing has changed at all except my perception of looking

at things or it may be the time that has changed. From sunrise to the sunset there came the moment to light up a lamp in my life. In the process to light up others I forgot that I too would need some lights to drive away darkness in my home.'

2.Location: A Mansion- Exterior, Day.

The cart stops in front of an old mansion. Banvari , the care taker of the house comes to pick up his baggage. Dayal steps down and moves quietly to his mansion. Banvari opens unlocks the door and requests him to proceed but he looks around for few moments to recollect his past.

3.Location: Mansion- Interior, Day

Dayal enters after some time to see many pigeons who made this house their home in his absence flutter around . He switches on the light and observes lot of dirt and cobwebs hanging from the walls. It looks as if the house has not been cleaned since he left it. The wings of pigeons drop down when they flutter to escape out of the room. Main credit titles appear on the wings falling down. He recalls his hey days with his family. Sound effects of pigeons fluttering and back ground music (Flash Back).

Shot division of the above scene:

1.Top angle, v/p cart, The pathway is left behind. The cart is running forward. Sound of horse hoofing.
2.Close up- Cart rider holds the reins of the horse.
3.Top angle. v/p of cart rider. Horse is running.
4.Close shot. Cart wheel moving.

5.Long shot. Cart is running on the pathway.

6.Close shot. Dayal in thoughtful mood.

7.Long shot Pan L/R. Cart running.

8.Top angle of the road leaving behind.

9.Close shot. Profile. Dayal is in thoughts.

10.Sunset.

11.Close shot. Dayal thinking.

12.Long shot Pan R/L. The cart moves out of the frame.

Monologue Dayal (from shot no.2-12): 'What a transformation of this place in few years or nothing has changed at all except my perception of looking at things or it may be the time that has changed.From sunrise to the sunset there came the moment to light up a lamp in my life. In the process of lighting up others I forgot that I too would need some lights to drive away darkness of my home.'

13.Long shot. Cart stops in front of the mansion. Caretaker helps him to step down and picks up his baggage. The cart return back.

14.Mid shot. Dayal stays for few moments to look at his mansion where he spent major part of his life.

15.Long shot Pan L/R of the mansion.

16.Close shot. Dayal looks at his house from left to right.

17.Long shot of the Mansion from Dayal's view point.

18.Mid shot. Dayal moves forward to the entrance.

19.Dayal opens the door. (door crackling effect).

20.Top angle. Long shot. Interior Mansion. Dayal enters in to a spacious Hall which had become home of many pigeons. They flutter around to escape. Dayal looks around the place which was unused for tears.

21.Pigeons in the process to escape drop their wings. The credit titles are superimposed on falling wings.

22.Top angle. Dayal switches on the light by pressing a button on the side.

23.Close shot. A light bulb covered in a shade turns out of focus for **'Flash back.'**

Few new comers in direction shoots a scene in many possible variations of shots so the Editor does not face a crunch of visual material. This may sounds to be a good strategy for a director but it has many drawbacks such as waste of time, money and raw stock to shoot extra length which may not be used by the editor. It also indicates lack of knowledge and experience of the director .In high budget films which constitute very negligible share of raw stock in the total expenditure, its wastage is not a concern as producers don't want to take a chance and the director too don't bother if he is sure of success of the film.

In a low budget film it is not only money that counts but also the professional reputation of a director which he would establish for himself during the course of the film. His lack of cinematic knowledge and technical indiscipline will be highlighted that may ruin his further prospects. He should take minimum and precise shots for a scene keeping editorial requirements in mind. The director may seek editor's cooperation in this regard. Few directors, who have an inclination for drawing, draw sketches of the first and the last frame of every shot. This brings clarity to shot compositions including their image size and the angles. These sketches reflect the needs of the director from other unit members too.

Scene construction:

There is always a purpose for an action or event which forms a scene. A scene without a purpose not only obstructs the flow of the story but also becomes a hurdle in its narration. There is no formula for constructing a scene or deciding the purpose of it in the screenplay. Flowing with the current of the story , writer divides his acts/sequences and events to create an interest. A scene is not effective without its pressing need to be included in the script. It is true that the screen play writer has to work very hard to conceive each scene which not only takes the story forward but is also interesting to make the audience tied up on their seats without allowing them to go out of theater for a puff. Every scene in the script is like a stair which should climb the audience step by step forward to its climax. A weak stair will demolish the entire journey of events and the characters in the story and the film will fall flat.

Purpose of the scene: why a character should come in and move out of the scene? It can be broadly defined with the purpose of entry or exit of the characters , brief introduction of the characters, mental state, psychological and emotional reactions, twist in the characters and the story, any other coincidences that require inclusion in the script. While constructing a scene or introducing a character the formula of 5 *Ws* and *one H* may be remembered by the writer to decide the inclusion and construction of the scene. ***The Five Ws are 'What, Why, Where, When and whom' and one H is 'How'.***

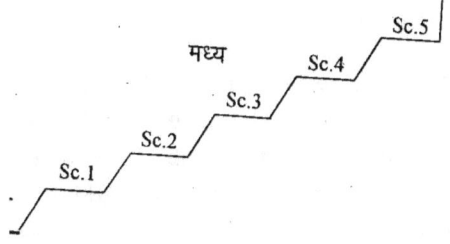

3.Climb to Climax

Dramatization :

A scene or an event that takes place in a simple and straight manner without upheavals may not generate an interest but if it is accomplished with lot of sufferings and struggles, hurdles and hopes, it not only achieve its purpose interestingly but also dramatizes the whole action. It creates more interest and anxiety in the audience to be more involved in the characters' actions and the events as a whole. Such dramatization makes a scene far more effective and entertaining than its simple and easy outcome.

Action and Reaction:

We are taught in our schools that when a ball is hit on a wall with certain force it bounces back with the same force. There is always a reaction of an action and same is an important factor in dramatization of a scène. The reaction generates confrontation, conflict and hurdles. If there is no reaction the action will be simple and ineffective and even may fail to invite attention. In conflicts and confrontations the powerful will be a victor and achieve his goal while the weak will break out but still may continue to fight for the cause till he is rendered

177

completely helpless.

It is not necessary to have a dramatic movement in every action and reaction however it depends on the importance of the event or the character that is able to bring some twists in the story. If there is more confrontation there will be more drama. There will be fewer dramatic moments in small happenings than the powerful and important events. Small events help the story move forward as every scene may not be powerful and dramatic. The writer should create as many hurdles and conflicts between situations and the characters as he can in the progression. Such moments of conflicts in the story display personal strength, mental state, psychological attitudes, the sincerity and objective of the characters. Nothing should happen easily on its own or by luck or miraculously. The scene construction must be based on the actions and reactions, events and accidents of the characters carefully crafted by the writer.

Dramatization is not meant to be starting from the beginning to the middle and the end of the scene. The writer may include some *'information'* regarding a situation or a confrontation passed on by someone at any point of time during the scene that is sufficient to create further conflicts of interest. A new character establishing his relationship with others can also be introduced in between if situation demands. This new character will provide links and the warning about forthcoming conflicts. A scene in a screen play is like heart in a body that has emotions and sentiments to move people further along with the story.

XXXXX

Scene 8:
Casting

Selecting an actor to suit a particular character for a film, stage play or a television series is immensely tough and challenging task. In the initial years of cinema most of the production studios engaged actors on their pay roll and the selection of a story was made to suit these actors . There were instances when the story was tailor made for an actor engaged by the studio. This continued for quite some time till the studio system declined. In this system entire unit worked as a 'family'. With the decline of studios when new actors made their entry in the industry it became bit difficult to find a popular actor suitable to the character as conceived in the screenplay. Moreover these actors lack dedication and group feeling in the working atmosphere as they are more in to money making than making a film. The problem of casting begins from the writing of screenplay as writers and the director don't know who would be playing their roles and how best they could integrate the mannerism of the particular actor in their characters. If the actor is known to play a specific role writer can mould and develop their character according to his personality. It makes developing a scene lot easier therefore before writing the screenplay director must keep the probable main actors in his mind about whom he knows and is sure that they will be able to do justice with the role. This is possible normally with high budget star cast or affordable popular actors in the films. In low budget films this may not be an important issue but director has to be extra careful while auditioning new actors and should not cast them unless he is sure of their talent that suits his requirement.

The cinematic ambience:

The ambience in cinema is the *artificial atmosphere* that is created especially for a scene to look realistic and authentic as we see and experience in our real life. Since most of the characters, situations and the events in the story are derived or inspired from real life, they are identified with the similarities in our lives as a film viewer. If we can't relate ourselves with what is happening on the screen, the whole purpose of the scene is defeated. Though an ambience may create a feeling of reality it is not complete in itself. It has to be supported by other cinematic means like the back ground, special or mood lighting, costumes of the characters, actors' looks and performance, Local language and culture, traditions and special occasions, festivals and celebrations etc.

On the stage, an actor creates an ambience by his special performance with the limited support of special stage lighting, sounds and the music. It is difficult for a theater director to create an ambience that is required in the act due to limited field and limited number of actors in the play. It is not so in cinema where sky is the limit for the director to create an ambience whether it is a war field or a crowded market place by erecting sets where artists can enjoy free movement in their performances. The number of people on the set/location may very from few to thousands depending on the requirement. Creation of a desired ambience is made easier by the use of digital effects where desired back ground or the crowd can be multiplied without actually employing it. The last journey of the Mahatma Gandhi in the film *'Gandhi'* by *Richard Attenborough* is still fresh in our mind where thousands of people were engaged to create an authentic ambience in the scene. A film camera too plays an important role with the use of different lenses and angles, special lighting and special effects.

Once the authentic ambience is created the actors too find it easy to get inspired and immersed in to their role to give an effective performance. The director too has an opportunity to modify his requirements according to ambience to inspire others to perform their best.

Casting director:

The process of selecting an artist is a joint effort of a producer and the director but if Producer is himself the director of the film he may engage a *'Casting director'* to help him . Casting director has a creative responsibility to search, find and coordinate with actors directly or through their representatives, secretaries and other agencies who deal with them. Casting directors have professional recognition whether it is for films, stage or television and they are now highly sought after professionals in the industry. Engagement of a casting director also relieves the director from this responsibility so he can concentrate more on the script and other issues.

Directors normally prefer to cast an actor with whom he has an affinity and confidence. It has its own draw back. The actor of his choice may not be appropriate for the character or the actor who is suitable for the role may not have proper equations with him. In such a situation director must display his maturity and take a conscious decision without forcing his choice that is favorable to everyone and try to make a balance between his selection and commercial viability. He should also display his skills to create understanding with other actors. While selecting an artist director must ensure that the actor meets the minute requirements of the character, his image and acceptability with the audience, acting skills and his behavior with people on the set etc. The final decision on the cast should be taken only after considering these parameters.

Budget of the film is another constraint while casting. A director may wish to cast a particular actor for a role but he may not have sufficient money to pay his fee. In this situation director must not immediately surrender to the situation and try to contact and convince the actor of his choice. Sometimes actors may not be fussy about their remuneration if the role is challenging and appealing that would satisfy their creative appetite. The director's own credibility in the field also plays a role in this selection however actor's secretaries or middle man may be an irritant in this regard.

'Billing', that is the place an actor gets in the credit titles, posters and other promotional material is another tricky issue that has to be sorted out with the actor before shooting. Billing reflects an actor's professional status, seniority, his success rating, the length and the importance of the role. There are no definite parameters for billing order but it has potential to derail the project at any stage till the release of the film. Every actor wants a prominent place for him in the billing chronology but sometimes it also becomes a major point of disagreement and conflict with other actors of similar star status. They don't want to be seen lower in ranking and inferior to others. Thus their billing position may be decided in

the early negotiations. It should be included as a clause in the agreement to avoid subsequent bickering.

Association of an actor with his director is much less in film than in the theatre therefore it is important for the director to establish his repo with him at the earliest. This will help creating comfort level with other crew members too. Few actors are expert in creating this comfort level with others sooner than others. Such actors are not only popular with their unit but are also preferred by producers and the directors to cast them in their next movie. An actor normally follows what director tells him as he knows that it is the director who knows best about the film so he would not like to cross his line. Such actors are called *'Director's actor'*. They don't interfere in the script and perform what is told to them and go for another shoot. These actors work in many films at a time and work in shifts. Contrary to this there are actors who take up limited number of films after a lot of thinking about their role, about the director and credibility of the producer. They put their best foot in their performance and like to ensure that the film is released and do business as per their expectations so they prefer to be kept informed about every development taking place in the production including screenplay writing, selection of co actors, length of other characters and its impact, Director's merit and sincerity, producer's professional standing and the distribution and marketing plan of the film. There is no time frame for completing a film with them so the producer should be prepared to let the tap of money unclogged.. If it dries up in the middle producer is doomed. They accept a film if everything falls in their line therefore it is difficult for a newcomer to work with such actors. They work when they are in a mood to work however no one can question their professionalism as they have a special place in the field. Dilip Kumar, Raj Kapoor, Dev Anand, Amir Khan, Feroz Khan, Manoj Kumar, Shashi Kapoor of Indian cinema have been the actors in this category.

The director should form an imaginative visual appearance, physical structure, behavior and mannerism of his characters while writing the script and try his best to match this imaginative picture of his characters with proposed actors for various roles. It may be remembered that a film character spends more time with his audience than his counterparts on stage do therefore there has to be a balance between the imaginative characters as perceived by the audience and played by actors. If there is distinct discrepancy and the characters seem far off the mark from the real life characters, they will not be acceptable. Many big budget films suffer due to this discrepancy where actors are (mis)cast due to their marketability but they don't believably resemble with their onscreen persona. It is also possible that an actor may not be perfect for a character and this perfection some time is impossible to achieve, in such a situation actors and directors should work hard to justify the characters they are playing.

Miscasting or inappropriate casting not only hampers the effectiveness of the film but also create imbalance in understanding and cooperation between actor and the technicians as they fail to establish a cordial functional relationship with the unit.. Actors feel neglected due to mismatch with their on screen character and others. This is a sign of disaster before film is completed and released. Therefore casting should be such that people on the set and outside start loving their actors. It also depends on performer's own acting skills and quality to influence others by his behavior. An actor should command appreciation for his performance and respect as a human being.

A director with dictatorial tendencies is another black spot on the set that is neither appreciated, respected nor followed by his actors or crew members until he has reached to such professional heights where no one has an authority to question his wisdom. Even such directors are not appreciated by the crew because film making is a team work and no one is above anyone. Everyone from top to bottom has the expertise to perform his respective job.

The film and television has gone through lot of transformation since its inception. The same is also true with acting styles. Actors of the earlier years were mostly influenced by theatrical style of loud and screaming dialogues to reach the last man sitting in the last row of the auditorium. Theatrical performance was evident in the films produced in the decades of fifties and sixties of the last century. Thereafter cinema production and exhibition influenced by the sophisticated recording and cinematographic techniques saw changes in acting style too which was away from its earlier avatar. Young and new comers in the field of acting now come in with their normal and natural flare of acting with in-depth understanding of the characters they play. Their family, educational background, their upbringing and their wide exposure to the world cinema also play crucial role to understand and analyze their characters that makes their performance plausible. Unlike earlier times the present generation of actors work to learn the nuances of cinema by attending a film school or by associating as an assistant director with some production unit before stepping in to the ring of film acting. This provides them practical knowledge of film making, intricacies of acting in front of camera and experience of working on a set with precision.

Stage actors:

It has been closely observed that performers coming from theater which is believed to be the *'mother of acting'*, find it extremely difficult to restrict themselves with in the camera field of a frame. Theater director has little control over the performance of an actor once he enters on the stage and he is free to act in his own style to reach the last man sitting in the hall by modulating his voice loudly and fast actions. The role of a theater director is restricted till the time of rehearsals. Another problem faced by the actor is that in theater he is used to perform his *'act'* continuously without breaks as a play is divided in number of 'acts' while in cinema an action is divided in numerous *shots* with a break in between the shooting of each shot therefore it is a challenge for a stage actor to act his scene in bits and pieces (shots)with in the limited camera field.

Actors on stage enter and exit as per their characters and perform mechanically due to its fixed area of visibility and action. It is not so in film shoots where the scene is not only divided in many shots but every shot has different perception and area of vision that is decided by camera angles and distances like long, middle and close to the object. These variations in the shots require an actor to perform and express his different emotions accordingly. The stage acting one can say is *'one take performance'* where the actor has to control his voice as well as his actions but in cinema actors normally have to concentrate more on their expressions and not on the quality of sound. Dialogues are dubbed later when he can improve his voice quality and modulations for proper emotional requirement.

The director must make sure before casting an actor from the stage if he would be comfortable to face the camera in its limited field. It is not necessary that an excellent stage performer also excels in front of the camera therefore the director may ask the actor to peep in to the camera view finder to see his field of movements. Similarly he should be explained the difference in Long, middle and close shots through the view finder. This will provide him knowledge about various camera fields before he really performs in front of the camera. This exercise may be done during the auditions. If director still finds him suitable he may be engaged. In this process the director comes to know the weaknesses of the actor which can be improved later with their proper understanding and opportunities.

An experienced actor is aware of the intricacies of stage and film acting so he can do justice to both and give his best performance. Acting is a meditation for such actors. They know that on stage action is **'shown'** but in cinema it is **'felt'**. They also know the difference in various types of shots therefore they control and express their emotions accordingly.

The film director must be a 'guide' to his actors and tell him when he is supposed to play down or exaggerate his actions. In cinema an actor is to behave like a normal character that reflects his own personality. During the rehearsals director should make sure that the actor assimilates and lives his character in him and not that he just plays it as himself. He should forget his personality and transform himself to the character he is playing and it is his success as an actor. The tendency to overact or loud acting by new comers in the field of acting should be strictly curbed and discouraged by the director.

Amateur actors:

Craze to become a film star blinds many of the youngsters to start dreaming to be on the film set without being prepared for it. The glamour of cinema takes them to board a train to the city where cinema is made. This leads them to immense sufferings and insecurities but they struggle to die than return back to their motherland. With the advent of many film schools and coaching classes many of them turn their heads to learn film acting. All film schools may not be up to the mark but something is better than nothing. These aspiring actors learn few steps of acting which could be a beginning in their career .Few get some small roles and short appearances on screen paving the way for a long journey. Few lucky ones with some connections in the industry get plum roles and few more fortunate who belong to a film family may grab the main role in an established banner.

Similar is the case with directors who may start as an assistant and climb the ladders in due course where some may take up directorial assignment in their home production without much struggle. They enjoy their preference to work with an experienced one or with an upcoming actor.

Few directors including me prefer to work with new comers in acting because these actors prefer to experiment and portray realistic characters unlike those who work with in their set image. Since these newcomers are not restricted to any stereotype image, director should take sufficient time, trials and auditions to cast them for a role which match with the image of the character he has formed in his mind that includes his physical appearance and structure, behavior and mannerism among other things required in a character.

I don't hesitate to confess that after being associated with documentary films for a long time, I am more inclined towards realistic cinema. Few years back when I was directing a short film *'Toote Pankh'*, on the issues and sufferings of senior citizens, I had formed an image of the lead character like that of *Anupam Kher* in the film *'Saransh'* and decided to cast him. My producer opined that if I cast Anupam Kher in this character people will identify Anupam Kher and the character of the film would be lost therefore he suggested me to cast a new comer for the role. I found myself in difficult mess as I had conceived and developed the character keeping Anupam Kher in mind. I was stressed to find a person who could match the image I had set in my imagination. I called many people for the photo sessions and the audition but I was not satisfied as Anupam became my obsession and the bench mark for my selection. With the time running out of my hand I toyed with the idea of shelving the film when I got a glimpse of an old man in his seventies in my complex when I returned home. He was chatting with people in the evening out. I did not know him nor did I see him earlier in my complex. I did not see him thereafter for many days but I was mesmerized by his appearance. I felt Anupam Kher was gradually melting out of my memories replaced by this man. I was sure that he would be the right person to play my character. After few days I discussed the issue with my wife Pratima and told her about this man. She too agreed and told me that he was a guest in our next block but the mute question was that whether a non actor could play the role which was so sensitive.

We went to meet him and told him about my intention to cast him. He agreed but said that he had never acted in his life except in his school days. I was enamored by his personality, his speaking, his behavior, his age and above all his visual image. After our brief discussion I was sure to cast him even if he never faced a camera. I told him to be normal in front of the camera and behave as he did normally. He need not act but remain as he was. With my interaction he was not only convinced but also developed self confidence to do justice to the character. He also came out of camera phobia. Thus Mr. Donde as he was called became Mr. Dayal of my film. My character Mr. Dayal was a retired govt. officer as that of Mr. Dhonde himself. Mr. Dhonde gave a memorable performance in the film that brought the character alive on the screen. So it can be true that with proper casting a non actor too can act in cinema.

Most of those who have been associated with reality films before migrating to fiction films prefer to work   with newcomers or non actors as they can be mentored the way a director wants. My docu- drama *'Toote Pankh'* and *'Wapsi'* were based on realistic themes and the main characters were played by non actors who resembled with the characters in my imagination. The word *'Docu drama'* was not common and not known to many, thereafter **'Docu drama'** became quite popular among film makers and the critics who appreciated reality films. The contemporary cinema has inspired and encouraged many film makers to attempt films on realistic themes who engage new or non actors to portray reality as it is. Another reason to cast new comers in such films is budgetary constraints and unguaranteed returns. A director finds it easy to establish cordial relationship with new actors due to no frills attached with their name.

Few directors claim that there is no difference between established and non established actors. sometimes newcomers may be more sensitive than established names and some established actors may not have the same sensitivity and impact on their audience. This is due to inherent talents a person is born with however a director has to make extra efforts to bring out his hidden merits. Another advantage with newcomers is that a director has more freedom to experiment with them that sometimes is not possible with big names as they carry their baggage of an image. It is not easy to break this established image for many reasons including commercial. Those names who dedicate them to their acting skills and not to their stardom only dare to break and carve out a new image which does not restrict them to stereotypical characters. When a director fails to get the desired performance from a new comer he can devise other technical methods including the use of symbols, close ups , montage and special effects to develop a scene. Where acting skills are considered it has been amply proved that new actors are much more successful in their performance due to their flexibility, respect for directors and a desire to experiment with their characters than their established counterpart. It becomes easier for a director to handle new comers when there is no dialogue for them in the scene. It applies to those actors too who behave normally in front of the camera as in real life. They find it difficult to speak predefined dialogues, they prefer to improvise their lines and speak extempore. The director should give them this much freedom. This helps an actor to perform in the best realistic manners.

Child artistes:

The main difference between adult and child artistes is that unlike adults children are not conscious about their personality, their behavior and mannerism, their actions and the camera. They do everything naturally. Some times their age becomes a problem when they start losing their natural flare when they grow. They become conscious of their behavior and start *'acting'* in front of the camera reducing the basic difference between them and the adult actors. Extrovert children in their subconscious mind do things naturally as directed but the director faces another situation when he finds it difficult for the child to repeat the similar action in case of a retake. Many times the child does not remember what he has done earlier therefore when dealing with children director should not depend on a retake nor should he expect it from a child artiste but try to finish the shot in the first take itself.

It is easier to cast a child artiste than an adult actor due to their easy availability. It is not appropriate to consider a child artiste a non actor because children can be more natural in front of the camera than their adult counterparts. They come out of their inhibitions and present a natural performance that may be difficult for an adult actor. While shooting with children director has to be very careful about their *'mood',* their likes and dislikes and deal with them politely with affection to avoid hurting them. Retakes, tough behavior, irritation may annoy a child that may hamper a take. The shooting discipline, punctuality and other requirements may be settled with the parents before signing an agreement for a child artiste to avoid shooting schedules to be in soup. Director also should try to accommodate child's needs and habits while planning a shoot.

Pre- shooting discussions:

Now the director is ready for shoots and everything is ready for a takeoff. By this time director must have read his script ample number of times and prepared a visual impression of his film in his mind but it is also the time to give final touches to the script. Once shoot is done nothing can be changed thereafter so the director must utilize this time to take his technical and other crew members in to confidence and involve them to discuss the scenes to be shot and invite their opinion if any. Some time there may come some valuable and unbiased suggestions from them. The director must listen to them with patience and consider their suggestions seriously. Pre shooting discussions with actors provide them clarity about their characters and an opportunity to improve their performance besides creating trust and cordial relationship.

Rehearsals:

Rehearsals are very common feature before a play is staged. In these rehearsals director tries to tie up all the loose ends and synchronizes various department in general and actors in particular . It is the actor who shoulders the responsibility of the play once he makes an entry on the stage floor where director has little control. It gives actors an opportunity to embellish their actions and movements. In cinema people have different opinions about the need for a rehearsal. Some believe that there should be rehearsal for the actors so that they avoid multiple retakes while few actors opine that rehearsing a scene again and again makes their performance stale and monotonous so they prefer to go directly for a take. They believe that their first take gives the best expressions and emotional display. This may be true with established actors and may not be advisable with upcoming actors who may waste lot of time before a satisfactory take.

Few actors like to rehears in their make room and finalize their dialogues, actions and expressions in the presence of selected unit members. It may be noted here that a rehearsal is not commenced only for an actor to decide about his actions and dialogues but is undertaken for the entire crew including cameraman, recordist, light men and the actors so rehearsals should be undertaken preferably on the set. No time frame can be fixed for a rehearsal as it all depends on the proper coordination between all the departments. One can proceed for a take once such synchronization is achieved. It may take few months of rehearsals of a play because director discovers new information about his characters and continues to improve them every day. It may not be necessary to devote long time to rehearse on a film set; even half an hour before shoot is sufficient. Actors may be provided copies of their scenes in advance to prepare themselves early and save time on rehearsals. Rehearsals with actors have another advantage that director gets an opportunity to convey his concept and emotional requirement of the character. Actors too try to understand his view point and work on their performance accordingly. The dictatorial directors don't allow their actors to perform independently while others give complete freedom to actors within their authority to display their acting skills so rehearsals also reveal the individuals attitude towards others.

It is normal practice for comedy actors to conceive their own dialogues and actions in consultation with director who may not have that much sense of comedy but comedy actors know what mannerism and dialogue would make their audience burst in to peel of laughter.

Similar is the case with those who play negative characters who conceive their own acts to give a new dimension to their characters. The comedy scene of the film *'Sholey'* (1973) directed by *Ramesh Sippy* is still fresh in the memories of cinema lovers whether it is the prison scene in which Jailor repeats his dialogues, **'I am a jailor of colonial times'** or **'My name is Soorma Bhopali'** still make people jump on their seats with laughter.

Film –Sholey
Scene No.
Location: outdoor, Prison, Time: Day
Characters: Jai, Veeru, Jailor, Warden, Police and other prisoners.

In the open space of the prison Jai and Veeru with prisoners stand in queue for a routine parade. Jailor enters with his police constables for an inspection.

Warden: 'Attention'.

Veeru: 'Chacha, when the parade stated…?'

Chacha: It is your first day today. You will come to know everything. The jailor is an obnoxious man.

Jai: 'He is coming.'

Jailor: 'Attention…'. **Jai and Veeru don't care for his order. Jailor gets annoyed.**

Jailor: 'I said –attention.'

Police: 'Sir, they are already in attention.'

Jailor: 'I know… I know… I know. Everybody listen me with open ears. Whatever has been happening in this jail will not happen till I am here… will never happen, No…no…no. I am a jailor of colonial times. I am not like other jailors of today who worry to reform prisoners. Ha…ha…ha…' **Jailor looks at Jai and Veeru and continues,** 'I know very well that you can never improve. If I could not change how you can change…ayn? I know people don't like me that's why I am transferred within few days from everywhere but in spite of so many transfers I have not improved, so remember and don't think that whatever you do, I will have no inkling about it. My spies are spread all over the premises. I get the report of every moment. Even a pigeon cannot enter here.' **A pigeon hits the eyes of the jailor and flies away. Jailor is shocked,**' o..o…o. what is it?'

Police: 'Sir. The pigeon.'

Jailor: 'What…?

Police: 'Pigeon…'

Jailor: 'something has fallen in my eyes. Take it out… leave it. It is enough for the day.. Now you all can go. Leave…leave.'

In this scene the comedy is not created by cheap antics but created by dialogues, personality of the character, his costumes, unique dialogue delivery, mannerism resembling to Hitler etc. The clone of Hitler reflects the toughness of the jailor on one hand but his careless persona, dialogues and actions reflect hollowness of this character. This contrast creates a situational comedy. Jailor is one of the main characters integrated in the story thus he becomes an integral part of the scene .The scene is not enforced but has an important place in the script.

Director should understand personal sentiments and merits of an actor and thereafter also understand the emotions of the character which he is to play and integrate them appropriately during the shoots. . If the personality of an actor resembles closely with his role, it becomes easier to create a realistic image of the character on screen. With proper understanding between actor and the director few changes if required in the development of the character, may be accepted. The involvement of screen play writer who has basically conceived these characters will be valuable.

Special traits for an actor:

There are some special traits required in an actor during the shoots such as jumping, swimming, horse riding, racing, driving, flying a plane etc. A professional actor normally trains himself in these skills before the shooting to avoid looking unreal. For others director should arrange such trainings before shooting and engage experts to remain present while these scenes are shot to ensure technical finish in the acts. Junior artists trained in these traits may be engaged for smaller or supporting roles however they may not be given any dialogue delivery in the scene. When the stunt is dangerous and main artistes may not take the risk to perform it , their *'duplicates'* may be used for the actions like accidents, fire etc. in the presence of experts. Close shots of duplicates or dummy artistes are not required.

Relations between an actor and the director:

The understanding and cordial relation between an actor and the director can either make or mar a cinematic experience. The actor on the stage performs independently after having in-depth grasp of the story, his character and actions, the director's requirements and expectations from him thereafter the director has little or no control on what happens on the stage. Actor's decision on stage is ultimate and no one can encroach between him and his audience during the enactment. He is responsible for the success or the failure of the play but in cinema relations between actor and director are of utmost importance as the success of the scene is not accredited to him but to the entire film crew in general and director in particular.

Beside the use of film technology like camera lenses, angles, special lighting arrangements and the ambience, an actor covers the distance between long shot and the close shots. Few actors may be more comfortable with long shots but others may prefer to express in close shots through their eyes, lips, wrinkles on the skin etc . Use of various lenses also restricts their acting abilities therefore it is desired that the actor may be shown the camera field of his action through the view finder. This exercise is helpful with those who face the camera for the first time so that their actions are within the frames. Unlike on the stage the actor in cinema does not know the pace and the rhythm of his actions which are decided by the editor by juxtaposing various shots at later stage therefore an understanding , cordiality and healthy relationship between an actor and the director is very essential to accomplish the desired out come.

An actor performs well when he is free of stress, apprehensions, lack of understanding, fear of criticism and ridicules about his work. They affect his performance therefore a director should maintain friendly and cordial relations with his actors and avoid their direct criticism. He should extend his guidance whenever he needs it. The few of the directors with their dictatorial attitude keep their actors stressed while few experienced actors and stars don't allow their directors to have their say particularly the new directors. Such situations are not congenial for a cordial relationship. The directors and the actors must have trust and feel secured in each other's company. This insecurity may create conflict between them. Some directors feel secured with established actors while few actors may be comfortable with new directors. Both these situations are not conducive to a successful film by any professional standards. They should get rid of such complexes at the earliest if they want to progress in their career. It may take some more time for a stage performer to adjust with cinematic requirements however with proper and regular guidance from the director they can do well in due course with dedication and sincerity .There is no need for a disappointment for them.

XXXXX

'Shot – The smallest unit (or building blocks) of the unbroken film. Shots are separated from each other by simple cuts and other kinds of transitions. They can be categorized by size and length. Most narrative films will count thousands of shots.'

Selecting a Location:

Choosing between an exterior set ,in the studios or shooting on actual location is one of the most difficult decision a director has to make while preparing for the shoots as both these options have their own implications. Shooting on a set whether it is indoor or outdoor, is far off from the reality though the art director in consultation with the cameraman and the director works hard to make it as real as possible but in spite of the best efforts by all, reality cannot be fooled by artificial creation. There are many limitations during shoots on a set, the biggest among them is the cost of erecting a set which is sometimes too high if the set resembles a palace or a fort or a railway station etc. Director therefore must make a thorough analysis and comparative cost study of either erecting a set or shooting on the real location. There are many studios that have created permanent sets commonly required by film makers such as court room, police station, temple, wayside market etc. In the Ramoji Rao film city of Hyderabad, India every conceivable indoor and outdoor location has been created for the shooting purposes.

There are many advantages of shooting on a set. It provides complete functional and creative freedom to the director and cameraman who can do special lighting for specific effect. There is also freedom to move the camera at will. Actors too get more time to prepare themselves for the shot in the privacy of their make rooms or vanity vans. The exterior locations whether indoor or outdoor have their similar pros and cons. In outdoor- interior locations director may have to make many compromises like shooting in limited space, restrict camera movements and actors too find crammed in limited area to perform their acts . In such situations director has to be contented with close shots or zooms. shooting outdoor-exteriors may be disturbed by unruly crowd and star fans who throng to have a glimpse of their favorite actors, lack of suitable permissions by local authorities, compromise in lighting arrangements, load shedding, lack of convenience and security etc. The director has to compromise in shot takings including his compositions. The Producers of films with high cost and stars prefer to erect an indoor or outdoor set in an isolated and well secured locations. The set of an entire village erected in outdoor locations for films like 'Sholey' and 'Lagaan' are still talked about. Indoor sets of *Paakiza, Mughal-e- azam* and *Devdas* (2001), *Bajirao Mastani* are highly appreciated. For a small budget producer, shooting in outdoor locations is his financial compulsion. Director must consider the budget and analyze the requirement of the script carefully before taking a decision on the location. If the director prefers to show reality and the budget is another constraint as is the case with many low budget films ,the director should never think of erecting a set. The theme based on fantasies, historical content and story revolving around palaces are generally high budget films with no restriction to construct a set as required. In fact it is appropriate to have a set for such films for the sake of convenience.

Selection of an appropriate location is   done after in depth understanding of the meaning, emotional effects and the message of the scene that director wants to convey to his audience. A Location appropriately earmarked accomplishes more than half of the vision conceived by the director.

The docu drama *'Toote Pankh'* directed by the author of this book *Kuldeep sinha* is a reflection of the traumatic life in old age, loneliness and isolation. I needed a location that symbolically become a mirror of boredom of the main protagonist Mr. Dayal who retired with many dreams to share and spend his old age along with his wife Janaki with their children. Their hopes are shattered and their life takes a different turn which they never bargained for. I wanted to establish and create the mood of aloofness right from the opening shot of the film. The sounds of horse hoofing coupled with the expressions of his feelings through Monologues reflected the waves of thoughts knocking at his mind. . I chose an isolated pathway of a remote country side where a horse cart is the only transport available to commute. The traffic on the road would have been detrimental to the isolation and feeling of loneliness of the main character. The setting sun indicated the return of people from the day's work. It synchronized well with Dayal returning home after few years of turmoil.

Home work:

Even with a perfectly written screen play and master scene script a director needs to assure him that everything is in line with his shooting plan. It is to ensure that all the preparations like setting, dialogues, shot division of the scenes are ready. It helps him to decide and review about the camera position angles, camera movements, artiste movement, special lighting if required, placement of properties etc. Once the set is ready, it's still photographs taken from different angles are useful for reference. After the review director communicates his decisions to his crew members. Such co ordination with unit helps him and others to refurbish their requirements and remove last minute glitches.

Many actors don't appreciate frequent changes in their dialogues and movements to avoid loss of concentration. It also hampers their predefined plan besides affecting their performance so proper home work helps director as well as the actors and other technicians to shed any confusion. This however should not restrict a director to incorporate some minor modification in his decisions on the set if need be. Who knows these minor changes may do wonders in the overall impact of the scene. Many directors undertake a dress rehearsal on the set with all his key unit members including his cameraman, assistants and dummy actors to finalize set lighting plan. Assistants are also tutored to prompt dialogues to actors from a predefined position to help them in proper delivery and timing. On the margin of the dialogues some assistant directors write the type of shots like Long shot, Mid shot or close shot along with camera angle and movement so as not to miss out anything at the end of the scene.

Before the shoots:

Amidst all the anxieties and hectic preparatory activities when the clock turns to the D day of the shooting, it is the time when a director is surrounded by his artistes, cameraman, art director and his lieutenants on the set or the location to realize his long awaited dreams to come true. He too wants to be sure of what he thought of, has been arranged in the same manners. It requires a meditative concentration of his entire crew. If the director delivers long winding sermons to his team, it breaks their concentration and creates confusion. It is not the time to tell them things which they have been or should have been told earlier. In fact people should be allowed to follow the guidelines and instructions they have been given during the discussions until and unless it is absolutely required to make some changes. With their long experiences and professionalism they normally understand what they are told earlier so there is no need for a repetition.

This is the time they all get things aligned for the take. The director of photography (DOP) places his camera and chooses an angle to compose the shot and rehearses camera movement with his assistants, electricians and studio boys fix lighting as guided by the lighting cameraman. Art director gives final touches to his set design and placement of properties. The sound recordist finds out position to place microphones in such a way that they are not visible in the shot. Actors too rehearse their movements with in the shot range. Director through the view finder of the camera finalizes the shot composition. In the new technology available today the director can see what is happening, composed and shot by the camera through a television monitor that makes it easy to suggest changes if required.

When all the technician are preoccupied with the preparations for the take, director is busy discussing dialogues, expressions, emotions and the movement with his actors. He considers suggestions, if any given by them. The purpose of this interaction with actors is to integrate them with their character. Actors try to give few variations in their dialogue delivery and movements as an option to the director to approve the best one of them. This in camera discussion with the actors is important to avoid unnecessary disturbance to the technicians preparing for the shot when actors too can concentrate in their actions.

Experienced actors are able to give their *first take ok* after few rehearsals but others in the shot may need more rehearsals and takes. In this situation the experienced actors start losing interest and become mechanical performer. They also lose their patience and their best performance while others improve with each rehearsal and take. This imbalance between actors has to be tackled very carefully and diplomatically by the director by calling the experienced actors after few rehearsals with others. *'Dummy'* of veteran actors may be used for such rehearsals to save them from boredom and exhaustion.

There is still no guarantee that the first or the second take would be Ok as there can be a mistake due to many reasons such as actors may forget their dialogues, they may fumble or give wrong movements, camera may stop, the lights may flicker or switch off, microphone may appear in the frame, outside sounds may disturb or something may spoil the composition during the take. Sometimes rehearsal or an Ng in retakes is better than the actual Ok take. Director must use his discretion to choose the best one in such cases. The director should neither be in hurry to go for a take until everyone is ready otherwise it may cause loss of raw stock and time nor should he loose his patience in case of retakes. He should work to make the atmosphere on the set as cheerful as possible.

Set Lighting:

Lighting is a very important and crucial factor in cinematography. In Hollywood the Lighting cameraman is provided equal rank and status to that of a cameraman. *'Exposure'* parameters are decided by the lighting cameraman based on the requirement of the scene, special style of the cameraman, the director and the *speed* of the film being used for the shooting. Special parapets for fixing lights are used in the height and the light stands on the ground level in a studio. *'Reflectors'* are used in outdoor shooting to reflect light from various sources including sun.

It is the responsibility of the lighting director to maintain **'consistency of Tone'** throughout the film. This measurement of light is done through an *'exposure meter '*or a *'light meter'*. Exposure meter is also used for measuring *'color temperature'* to balance various colors with the help of *'color filters'*.

Shot composition:

We all know by now that the action in a scene is divided in many shots. When these shots are joined together they recreate a continuous action of the scene. The way a sentence is composed by joining different words, similarly different shots when juxtaposed create a scene. A shot is a *'Unit'* for the scene.

The prominent role in the *composition* of a shot is played mainly by the director and the cameraman who decide about the camera placement, camera angle, image size or the distance of the camera from the object, camera speed including the variation required for a slow motion or fast motions, artiste's movement and their performance etc. In cinema a picture not only moves but talks too to create more emotional impact. Special lighting in the shot is another device to enhance this impact.

One should remember that a moving picture is a series of still photographs exposed in film frames. These still frames are given special meaning by the creative vision of a cameraman and the director. Everything happening in the frame is always not be seen ,heard or felt completely by our eyes or ears. A film frame is much more sensitive than our senses. The composition of a shot is a reflection of what a frame contains. The frames are decorated by various means such as special lighting, property, set design, colors of the furnishing material, fixtures and the camera and actors' movement. A film frame for a cameraman or a film director is what a canvass is for a painter who plays with colors. Similarly in a film frame the director and the cameramen create visuals which impact our senses and sentiments.

It may be noted that nothing happens within a film frame without knowledge and approval of director, even a bird can't fly across the frame without a purpose. Shots not only convey a new meaning when juxtaposed together but also offer different interpretation to the scene. Shots are a means of communication between the film maker and the audience to enable them to think on the same plane and wavelength as that of the director. When audience understands the same what a director wants to convey them through these shots, it is the success of a director.

Type of shots:

The distance between camera and the subject or an object defines various types of shots. This distance is decided to create different compositions, effects and emotions. The director and the cameraman divide the scene in many shots maintaining continuity of actions and dialogues. Every shot has different meaning and interpretation which is expressed in different size of images and angles of the camera placement .

Every shot and camera movement has a purpose so a shot needs a great care while being composed. This is explained in the following pages.

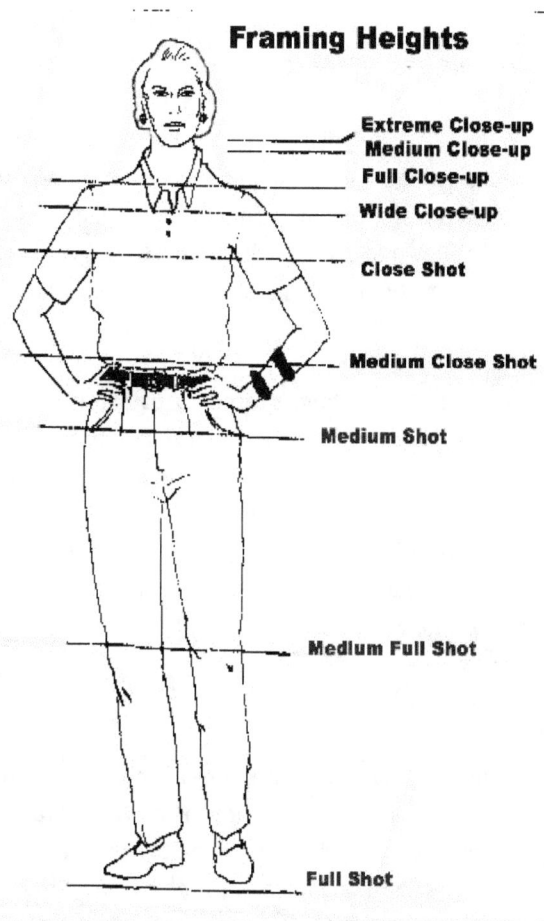

3.Sizing of the shots

1. Extreme Long Shot (E.L.S.):

ELS is generally used to establish a wide spread outdoor location where an action is supposed to happen or the back drop of the story or a scene. This shot is also called *'Establishment shot'*. For example if the back drop of a scene is a dessert, a ELS will register an image of a wide spread desert in the mind of audience and they will understand that it is the place where entire story will be evolved. ELS can be taken from a top angle from the helicopter, airplane, hill top or a rooftop to show the area as wide as possible. War fields or a huge procession or density of crowd etc are established in ELSs.

Symbolically ELS is creatively used to establish isolation or loneliness, depression, inferiority or insignificance of a character etc. People in the theatre immediately know about his mental state, social status or depression of the character and identify with him. While a character is established in ELS, action is normally avoided because of its poor identification in the extremely long distances.

2.Long Shot (L.S.):

A *Long shot* clearly establishes place and an action on a location. Unlike in ELS, an action or a character has comparatively better visibility due to reduced distance between camera and the subject. LS too are used to establish the location or the backdrop of a scene. In LS less attention is paid to the atmosphere and the surrounding area but to the character or action, the background, ambience, setting or natural surroundings, properties. Undesirable people, characters or action are avoided in LS. Therefore long shot should be carefully composed with proper atmosphere, properties and lighting arrangements. Character movement in long shots looks slower so the length of an action should be short.

3.Long shot

It is normal for an actor to move from the distance to close or close to a distance during his performance. It is called '**long shot to close shot'** or vice versa in the same shot. In this situation the action, background, ambience, actors' actions and reactions can all be seen in a single shot. When a character comes close to the camera he gains importance and when someone goes away from the camera he loses it.

3.Mid Long Shot (M.L.S.):

It is the distance from head space (a margin between the head and the background) to the knees of a character.

4.Mid Shot (M.S.):

In this type of shot, objects and the area around the subject or the character is excluded. It is basically a '***Body shot'*** where body of a person is kept in the centre to establish relationship between various characters without minute expressions and emotions. Mid shots are widely used in dialogue sequences.

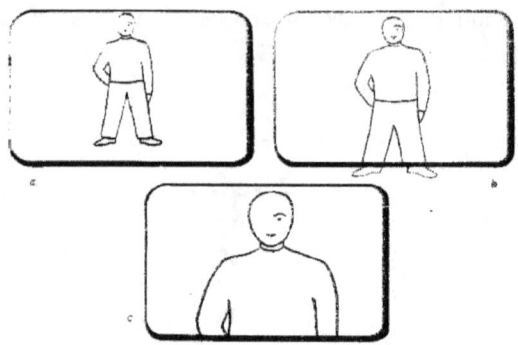

5.Long shot. Mid Long shot, Medium shot

5.Medium Close Shot (M.C.S.):

MCS covers the distance between chest and head and is generally used for conversations. MCS is easy to juxtapose with any other shots like MCS to CS or vice versa to bring variations in effects. During the conversation MCSs can also be taken from **over the shoulders (O.S.).**

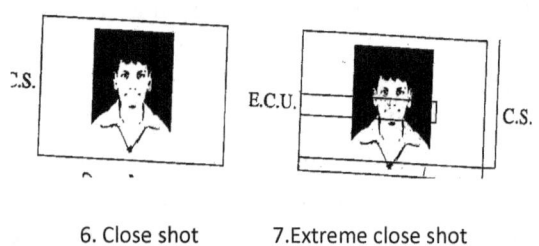

6. Close shot   7.Extreme close shot

6.Close Shot (C.S.):

Close shot is considered to be most important shot in film making that takes the audience close to a subject or the object. It exclude everything around a character including the ambience or the background. Close shots are little closer to head and shoulders than the *Mid shot*. It concentrates on the face where importance is given to emotional expressions and facial reactions of the character. Variety in close shots can be obtained by changing camera positions and the angles. The coordination of moods, lighting and camera position is important while taking a close shot because of limited background and other details. Closer the camera to the face wider is the image size in a close shot in which other details are eliminated. Zoom or trolling to close shot creates better dramatic and visual effects. There has to be a complete coordination between camera position, its height, eye levels , tilting, lighting and the mood while composing a close shot to avoid camera consciousness . Director has to be extremely cautious when taking CS as they should not be taken if there is no facial expression. Close shots are effective in displaying emotional expressions, built up of the climax and creating drama in the scene. Close shots can be juxtaposed with any shot as *'inter cut'* during the editing.

7.Extreme Close Shot (ECS):

They are useful to express minutest emotions, feelings and better dramatic effect. ECS are effective in creating suspense and mystery. Director and the actors must be sure of the needs and utility of ECS otherwise ECS will look unnecessary and forced in the scene. In ECS smaller and minute details of an object are magnified such as eyes, lips, finger thus it is used to create dramatic effects.

Every type of close shots creates different and deep impact therefore ECS are taken with extreme caution when required. One should avoid excessive use of '**close up**' which are also not related to preceding or following content (shots). Close shots are extremely useful for television due to its small screen size. Long shots are rarely used but even in television every shot should have a purpose and the meaning when used.

In addition to the above mentioned '*composition shots*' there are few more type of shots that are used for different purpose and narratives for editing purposes-

8.Cut away shots:

As it sounds by its name *'cut away shots'* divert the attention of audience from the ongoing scene or action for a brief interval. The cut away shots are generally not part of the main scene or action, for example the shots of crowd intercut between racing event to make it more interesting. The reaction and cheers by people in the stand during the race enhance excitement of audience and creates curiosity and anxiety about the final outcome. Sometimes cutaway shots are used to represent viewers point of view and reactions. Reaction of another person in a conversation scene between the two is a cutaway shot that can also be called '*Reaction shot'*. Cutaway shot sometimes present a symbolic similarity with other subject or an object , for example a simpleton is juxtaposed with a rabbit or a dancer is juxtaposed with a dancing peacock.

9.Additional shots:

They are normally part of the scene but taken in addition to the predefined shot division of the scene. They are generally taken as an alternative to the main shots and are used when a scene needs some extension of time or to create some more drama in the scene or repeating the same for recall purpose at later stage. Since *'Additional shots'* are part of the scene they should be used only after establishing the scene or the location by *'establishment shots'* otherwise they will be irrelevant and will obstruct the flow and effect. Additional shots are generally used by the director to emphasize the visual and dramatic effect by extending the centre of action. This can also be done by using zoom lens or trolly but a direct cut is always better for this purpose. While taking additional shots the continuity of previous action , looks of the artistes and their movements should be kept in mind. The close shots should be different from the view point of the mid shots otherwise the editor may find it difficult to feel a cut between them.

Most of the additional shots are taken after the main shoot is over so actor too should remember their action continuity, camera position, angles and their looks to the camera. Cameraman while looking through the view finder should also ensure that actors' look properly to the specific direction. Additional shots can also be used in between a lengthy shot to reduce the action or the time lapse.

In the documentary or educational films director should be aware about the specific *focus points* which he would like to emphasize and how could he present them more interestingly. Additional shots are helpful in maintaining a particular pace and rhythm by reducing or extending the screen time of the scene. Screen time can be reduced by cutting the length of the shots and may be increased by extending this length, repeating or adding additional shots. In the information films this length is extended or reduced to match the narratives.

10.Inserts:

They are very useful for an editor when he finds some continuity jerks and flaws while juxtaposing the shots. For example , if there is a jerk in looks of two characters in conversation , a camera rumbling or a technical glitch, an insert solves the problem when it is used to replace the unusable portion in between the take.

Inserts can also be a cutaway or additional shot taken for the scene. The length of the inserts is very short. Normally they are not part of the main action but can be used to create ambience, for example when there is a party an insert of the activities in the kitchen or in the bar will show the parallel action going on in the adjacent room. While this is not directly connected with the scene, it is used to create an atmosphere.

Inserts also come to rescue when the editor wants to cut down extra length of a running shot , shortening a long camera movement or an action. There will be a continuity jerk when a shot is cut in between; an insert at the cutting point makes the transition flawless however the insert should belong to the same scene. This insert can be a reaction shot, a close up , shots of some property that is already established in the scene earlier such as a telephone, wall clock etc.

When these shots are juxtaposed with another the great care has to be taken to maintain *'continuity of action, continuity of thoughts, continuity of emotions and continuity of compositions* that includes action, movements, looks of the artistes through the camera, magnification and angles of the shots etc. The wrong juxtaposition not only disturbs the mental flow of the audience but also jerks in the physical actions on the screen. Though there are various methods to manage *'continuity'*, the director and the editor , cameraman to certain extent must have the knowledge of its implications and the solutions without disturbing the flow.

Composing a Shot:

Every subject or object that is visible in the image of a frame is a reflection of imagination of the director and the cameraman. It is similar to that of artiste who translates his imagination of colors in his canvas. Cameraman and the director both work hard to recreate their vision of the film on the canvas of celluloid as attractive and effective as they can as we all want to see beautiful things around. Modern cinematic techniques and lenses help a great deal to recreate beauty in the frame.

There are many different types of lenses available such as Wide angle lens, Telephoto lens, Macro lens, Zoom lens etc in addition to the normal lenses varying from 16mm to 75mm that are part of the camera accessory to make the image more effective. Special lenses are available on demand while normal lenses come along with camera set up. Zoom lens generally takes care of most of the requirements of a cameraman in which one has just to change the focus.

Zoom lens is capable to take many varieties of shots from a single position by changing the magnification of the images. Shifting focus multiple times in a single shot may be a creative urge of a director or a cameraman , it should be practiced only when there is absolute requirement in a shot as it is not only time consuming but risky to have multiple focus in a shot. It may result in blurring of shots if the assistant involved in follow focus is not confident and experienced enough.

The type of lens to be used in a shot is purely a cameraman's prerogative considering the concept and setting .The director generally should not interfere in his discretion so the director should concentrate on the composition of shots instead of deciding the type of lens or lighting etc. Composition of a frame depends on the creativity of the cameraman and the art director. If the director himself is operating the camera, it is he who should do it otherwise director must leave the operative cameraman to do his job independently.

While composing a shot decision about an angle that gives specific magnification to the image and the effect is another crucial task before a cameraman. The image size and its effect jointly give an identity to the shot therefore the selection of an angle and image size has to be done very carefully to complement the desired impact that the director and the writers have envisioned. It may be noted that every size and the angle has different effect and purpose therefore their selection should be such that displays the specific emotional expressions. Selection of a lens, an angle and an image size reflect creative and professional merits and maturity of director and the cameraman.

Many of the directors and the cameraman indulge in unrestrictive use of a zoom lens to save time and raw stock without considering the character of the shot , to speed up the pace of the scene. It should be avoided as the excessive use of a zoom lens neither enhances the impact of the scene nor it serves any purpose but has another danger of being stressful to the eyes. Zoom lens has a specific purpose of highlighting a characters emotions and the expression which should be appropriately understood by them and use whenever it is required.

The lenses:

A camera comes with variety of lenses of different focal lengths that serve the purpose of taking shots of different image sizes . There are few *standard lenses* that come as accessories with the camera while few other special lenses like wide angle, telephoto, macro and zoom lenses are to be demanded separately. The lenses with Short focal lengths are used for taking Long shots and higher focal length are used for close shots.

Focal length/Lens angle:

The angle of the lens is normally fixed at the horizontal or eye level as our eye sees an object either horizontally or vertically. Similarly through the lens we can see only a limited area however this field of vision can be widened or reduced by the use of different type of lenses which provide different size of images. The angle of a lens depend on the specific requirement of the director so he should ensure before deciding about the use of a lens and the angle that all the actions in the shot take place in horizontal or vertical limits only. The activities taking place outside this limit will not be visible or they may be distorted. The clarity in various image sizes is according to focal length and the angle of the lens.

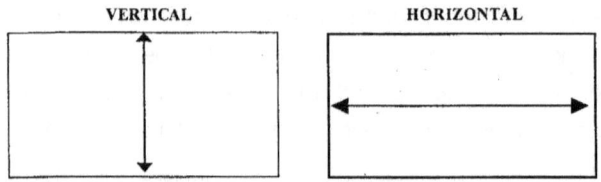

8.Horizontal and vertical planes

Suppose an object is positioned at a definite distance from the camera and there is a choice to select one of the available lenses. The lenses of various focal lengths will produce different image sizes in the same distance. According to a simple thumb rule **'Lenses of less focal length cover wider field of vision while the lenses of higher focal length will capture less area.'** It means that a long shot will require a lens of less focal length and a close shot will need a lens of higher focal length.

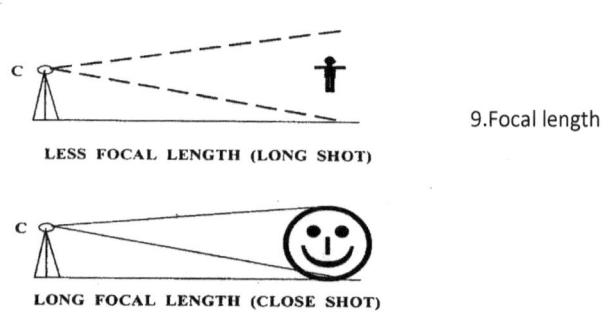

9.Focal length

Depth of field:

The entire field including fore ground and the background that is visible without distortion from a focal point is called **'Depth of field'**. The depth of field depends on various variable factors such as focal length, aperture setting, distance between the subject and the camera, intensity of light, film speed and the type of raw stock etc.The depth of field is increased if-

1. Aperture is reduced while focal length and the distance between camera and the subject remain constant.
2. When the camera is shifted away from the subject without changing the focal length and the aperture.
3. Focal length is reduced while aperture and the distance between camera and subject remain constant.

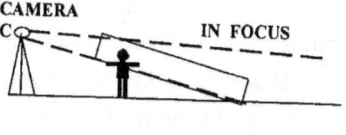

10a. Depth of field

According to a general rule if aperture is less depth of field is more. Opposite to it if aperture is more depth of field is less and superficial. In the bright illumination cameraman is more comfortable to define the depth of field as per the requirement of the director but it creates problems for him when director requires more depth of field in less illumination. In case of shooting in less illumination or in dark a *'fast emulsion film'* or a *fast speed film* can be used to reduce superficiality in the depth of field. Fast speed film requires much less illumination. Generally fast speed film is helpful in night shooting or where there is less light available.

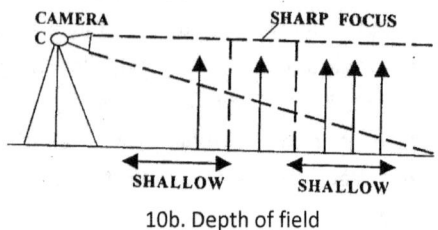

10b. Depth of field

Better visual effects can be obtained with wide aperture and reduced depth of field. Medium or close shots of actor can be taken separately for creative and dramatic reasons.

For various technical reasons there is always a need for an in depth discussion between cameraman and the director prior to the shoots. It is not necessary that director briefs the cameraman about a particular lighting arrangement or the use of a specific lens. It should be left to his discretion however the director must ponder about the following questions and know their answers with clarity. It helps him to organize a proper scene.

1. If he wants to see everything in the shot clearly or if he wants all the characters, places or their portions appearing in the shot to be clearly identified by the audience? If yes, then the director requires entire depth of field to be in sharp focus.

2. Does he want to establish relationship of all the characters in the frame?

3. Does he want to emphasize a particular object or specific character on the screen?

4. Does he want to establish the relationship of action occurring in the foreground and the background? This also depends on the location where many actions take place simultaneously on different spots.

Selection of a lens becomes more crucial when there are two or more characters in a frame. Wide angle lens increases the distance between two characters therefore with appropriate angle and camera placement relations between each character can be properly established.

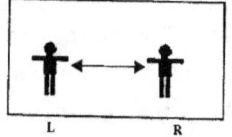 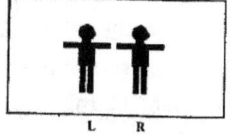

11.Wide angle distance   12 Normal distance

In the first illustration wide angle lens nullifies the image size by increasing the distance in the relationship between two characters thus giving importance to the right one. In the another illustration telephoto lens reduces the gap and the size. In this situation viewers' attention will be more towards left one between two characters. The problem is more acute in over the shoulder shots when two characters face each other. A distortion of distance or image size between them created by telephoto lens will be unnatural and their relationship may be questioned. With the change of lenses emphasis may be shifted from one character to another. Telephoto lens should not be used to reduce distance between two characters however other methods can be used to achieve it such as variety of lenses, lighting arrangements, set compositions, movement of characters etc. Characters standing in equal distance will not be interesting unless they are involved in a meaningful and effective conversation that emphasizes a particular character. Such shots should never be taken lightly as there is deficiency of creativity and special effect.

Lighting :

Lighting for a shot reflects creativity of a cameraman and the director. Most of the cameramen prefer to involve themselves in lighting . With the exception of realistic films most of the commercial cameramen indulge in over lighting or excessive lighting to show the set or a shot well lit up. They do it to avoid lighting for each shot separately and to be sure that every shot is clearly seen. In this process they forget that every shot needs a different lighting according to its mood and requirement. This general lighting neither serves any specific purpose to highlight a character or an object nor does it create special effect or moods therefore lighting of a set should be to create an interest, attention and emotional effects of the characters while ignoring unwanted details.

Excessive set lighting spoils the space used for the shot and negates the balance between light and shades. Excessive lighting is normally seen in television programs due to their small screen size and lack of depth. It is not proper to go for excessive lighting in motion pictures where screen size is many times bigger and depth of field is more. The director and cameraman who are fascinated by over lighting face many problems in composition of a shot.

Shift of Focus:

When the director wants to shift attention from one person to another in a single shot ,**'shift of focus'** from one subject or object to other is executed. This shifts the attention to another object or character. Shift of focus technique is normally applied in promotional or advertising films but many of the directors use it as a visual gimmick. Shift of focus should not be done without a purpose or a reason, otherwise it becomes a misadventure. Normally focus shift may be done only when there is more distance between two subjects and the other is beyond the threshold of depth of field. when the distance between two subjects is less ,the shift of focus will not only be invisible but will also be ineffective. Director may emphasize an action in the foreground by keeping the background out of focus or he can remove a person or portion in the background by keeping them out of focus to give importance to the foreground.

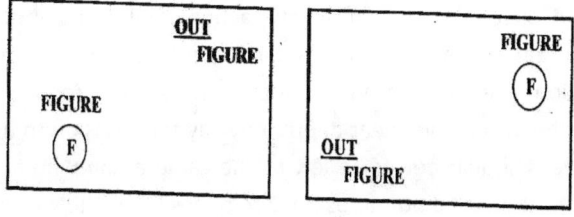

13.Shift focus

Zoom lens:

Zoom lens is generally used to reduce the foreground and move closer to the subject. Zoom lens has come in to practice since the third decade of twentieth century which was an adolescent period of cinema. Thereafter by the fifth decade of the last century it has become very popular among film makers and it became a fashion to use it everywhere and anywhere. Many people still are not aware of the possibilities of its application. Unfortunately most of the cameramen inappropriately use zoom lens for tracking or a trolly shot.

Zoom lens is very convenient and useful for shift focus shots due to its easy operation. It can shift focus multiple times from and to an object without standard lenses or with a multiple lens turret mounted on the camera. It makes it more comfortable for the news reel coverage. Zoom lens reduces the distance between the camera and the subject and captures the action without shifting from its position. It otherwise would require different lenses and camera placements.

Zoom lens is not considered appropriate for shooting a moving object or action due to distortion in pictorial depth. Without pictorial depth the follow- action will lose its impact and appeal however zoom lens can be used to highlight the distortion in depth for dramatic or creative reasons. Zoom lens should be avoided in linear depth. Anyway the decision to use zoom lens should better be left to the cameraman who may take a cautious decision to use it. Zoom lens takes the viewers close or away from the subject from a static camera position but one should generally avoid zoom without purpose.

Excessive zoom in to subjects do not serve any purpose and are stressful to the eyes.

Lens and the movements:

The lenses used in camera have an intimate connection with the set, location and the action taking place in the scene. The purpose of pre shooting rehearsals is to select the appropriate lens for the action in the shot. The lens required for a shot can vary in different locations/set. If the place is small the lens needed to shoot an action will be different from the location which has wider area or in the outdoor locations. If the same action is shot in a studio there will be another lens requirement. Movable walls are used some times in a studio to help cameraman select an appropriate lens and move his camera comfortably. If an action is shot in a small room a normal lens may be used but the same action in outdoor location will require wide angle lens. Sometimes for better visual clarity and minimum distortion, an actor's movement is deliberately kept slow. It happens when the actor has to move towards or away from the camera.

Telephoto Lens:

Shooting of the same action in different location with different lenses establishes the relationship between the lens and the action. If the actor moves towards the camera and his movement is to be seen slow for some dramatic reasons, a telephoto lens will be used. This slow movement is caused due to the visual distortion created by telephoto lens which cannot be corrected by any means. If telephoto lens is used without a dramatic requirement, it will create irritation and distortion will be an avoidable hurdle. Similarly a telephoto lens when used for fast paced event like sports and news events etc, it will dilute its effect by slowing down the normal speed of the action. A telephoto shot needs to be stayed on screen for a longer time than its real time, it becomes a hurdle in the normal pace of an action. Telephoto lens also does not give decent result when used to shoot athletes running in a row therefore the choice of telephoto lens should be a conscious decision prior to the shoots after a serious consultation between the director and the cameramen.

Distortion:

All the lenses except normal lens create visual distortion to a certain degree. This distortion if used creatively for a dramatic purpose gives decent result otherwise it is not more than a mere visual jugglery. The director should acquire knowledge about the possibilities to use variety of lenses before he takes a decision about the impending effect of an action and his choice of lens should corroborate the requirement of the scene.

Camera angles and placement:

The audience watches a film with their perspective what is shown to them on screen by the director. Every character in a story has his own perspective about other characters and the situations which is expressed by his various actions, reactions and the movements. This perspective of characters becomes viewers' perspective when they watch them perform on the screen. The audience begin thinking, reacting and expressing the way those screen character do implying that what director wants them to see, think and do, the audience starts doing the same. It means that the perspectives of the director and the audience have integrated well and this emotional integration is continued till the end of the film. Lenses, camera angles and camera placement play very important role to facilitate the expression of this perspective of the character and the director. Every angle represents a special situation, relationship between the characters, their emotional state and reactions, importance of the character in the scene etc so the director must attain the knowledge of all the lenses and their effects if he wants to communicate in the right perspective what he wants to.

Height:

Normal height of camera placement is the height of an individual which is generally considered up to **eye level**.

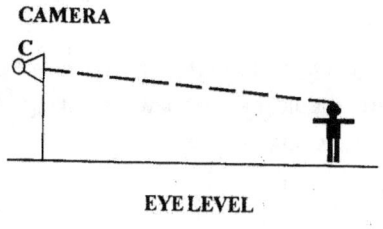

14.Eye level

When camera is placed in low angle it looks up at the higher level and when it is in top angle it looks at lower level. Low angle and top angles in the camera are important to create dramatic effects but they should be sparingly used when needed.

Top angle shot:

Camera in *Top angle* is positioned above eye level and tilted down. A top angle shot of a character reduces his importance and shows him as weak, timid or powerless. A top angle taken from wide angle lens presents highly dramatized panoramic view of a wide and scenic locale. Top angle shots are very useful in the coverage of sports' events such as football or cricket matches. Top angle shots are two dimensional so the landscapes from the extreme top angle are separated to planes, forests and rivers etc and the cities will look in linear or squire   shapes..

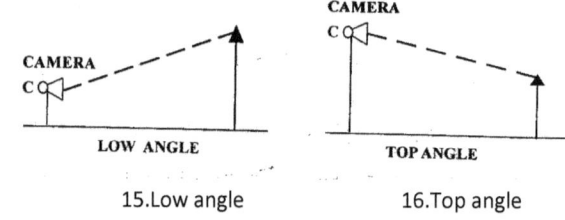

15.Low angle   16.Top angle

The close shots in top angle or low angle have lot of visual distortion so care should be taken while taking close shots from top angles or low angles.

Low angle shot:

In *Low angle* camera is placed below eye level and is tilted up. The viewers in a low angle shot have a feeling to see upward. The character in low angle gets emphasis and importance, seems to be powerful and strong in comparison to others. A low angle shot taken from a wide angle lens may instill fear in the mind of the audience therefore such shots are taken to dramatize a scene or create scare in a thriller film. Low angle cuts out or completely removes the unwanted space around the person that's why these shots are more useful in outdoor location where director has no control over the situation.

Normal view point:

It has the least dramatic effect. In fact there is no effect except visual expressions. It does not change perspective. Distortion too is minimal so the scene looks normal in view. It means that horizontal and vertical lines will be normal. Here director has to decide if the character has his subjective view point; camera position will be at eye level. This shot represents the view point of the character that also becomes the view point of the audience so the shot will be taken by placing camera at eye level.

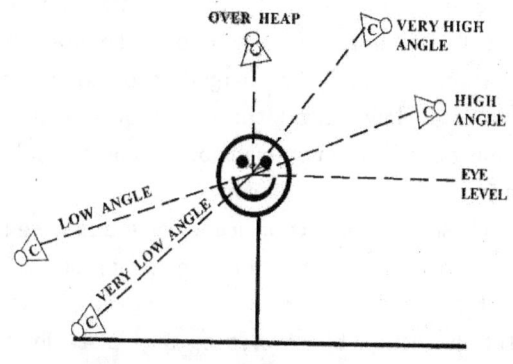

17.Various camera angles

Camera slanting:

To show an object in diagonal or tilted position camera is placed down below or above eye level in tilted position. Though it does not serve any purpose, such slanting shots are taken by the cameraman or director as a variety and decorative piece. Generally such shots are taken in action sequences or swift actions. Slanting shots represent swift action, violence whether human or natural such as earth quake, floods, volcano or a particular type of emotion. These shots easily attract attention of the audiences so are used commonly in advertizing films. Slanting shots are used in educational films to make them more interesting. High rise buildings,Hills and subjects at the height are intercut with characters to make the scene dramatic and exciting.

Camera positions:

A camera position has the most intrinsic relationship with the action and the frame where action enjoys more importance in the two, whether it is a highly charged action and dramatized fiction film or a low budget short or a documentary film. Director must brief his cameraman about camera position only after having understood and convinced about the desired effect. While shooting an action scene camera may be moved closer to the place of action and not the action be performed in front of the camera to keep the normalcy of the action intact. Let the action be allowed to take place in its own normal form and the camera position may be decided according to its need.

Once the relationship between the camera and the action is understood properly a decision about its placement and the lens to be used may be taken considering the rhythm of other shots in the scene. For example in wide angle an actor will be walking faster than in the long focus lens therefore his walking speed has to be regulated in such a way that it matches with other shots of the similar action.

If there are many characters in a scene they all should be shown busy in some activities instead of standing like lamp posts. Activities of these background characters may be clearly defined prior to the shot. The eye line continuity is another important factor when there are many characters in a single shot. There direction of looks should be properly monitored and maintained. However junior artistes or extras may be left on their own and concentration may be paid to the major characters. They should be briefed about their direction of looks while doing rehearsals.

Pan shot:

When the camera is moved on its axis from left to right or right to left ,it is a '**Pan shot**.' The word *'Pan'* is derived from *'Panorama'*. Its purpose is to make viewers aware about the background of the scene. Pan shots are of the following types-

1.Survey Pan: This shot introduces the place of event when the audience imagines the area of the events, natural surroundings and the forthcoming events. He tries to understand the linear and aerial perspective of the area and the detailed characteristics of the place. Survey shots are generally used in the beginning of the film to establish the place where story will unfold.

2.Tracking Pan: In this shot camera centers around a moving object, character or an action from left to right or right to left for example; pan on a moving car, train, horse race, man walking on a road etc. In tracking pan shots these actions are centre of attention that take the story forward. Such shots are taken in the overall perspective of the scene. The speed of a tracking shot should be similar to the speed of moving subject otherwise it will be difficult to consistently maintain its central position in the frame. The subject will be moving in and out of the frame and the cameraman will be shifting his camera to catch it left and right. This is a frustrating situation for audience and the cameraman therefore the speed of camera and the moving subject should be constantly maintained and matched with the composition and the speed of the next shot to avoid speed difference in similar type of action in the same scene. Tracking shot with telephoto lens should never be attempted as it creates vibrations and distortions in the shot that is completely unacceptable.

3.**Slow and whip Pan:** The speed of a pan shot is decided on overall pace of the scene and its purpose. Slow pan in the beginning creates curiosity of the audience about the next scene however in the end when other characters are included in the shot the center of attention is shifted to the characters, objects or the action. Opposite to it the whip pan, fast pan or swift pan as it is called is used as a transition device in a fast action or change of a scene or to create blur effect to dramatize a situation.

Moving subject:
Cinema is defined as *'Moving images'* that are seen on a film screen or television. These movements are created by the

movement of camera, action of the actors or the moving objects. This is done to create *'illusion 'of reality'* because in our day to day life we hardly see anything static whether it is time, events or actions taking place around us or our thought process and emotions, they are all full of drama. ***'The world is a stage and we are all actors performing our defined roles'*** the quote might have been inspired by this fact. It is reality and an illusion of this reality is created on cinema screen therefore it is necessary for us to see, hear and feel that looks real. This illusion is not the result of the efforts of a cameraman or the director but is created by the chronological juxtaposition of shots by the editor. To achieve it, it is necessary for the director to create an inherent pace of the scene according to its emotional value. The speed in an emotional scene will be slower than in the action scene. This speed is decided jointly by the director and the cameraman while constructing a scene This speed is created by the camera movement and the action in front of it. They both should commensurate with each other. An action in front of a still camera will not be interesting and will lack dramatic elements. In contrast a moving camera following an action will be more interesting, attractive and dramatic. In such shots camera becomes part of an action. Camera plays a significant role in composition of a shot however choice of a lens and the speed should be carefully made. Whether an action should be in long shot or in a close shot is decided according to inherent emotions and the mood of the scene. Therefore director must be very clear about his scenes and the requirements that he should extensively discuss and communicate with his cameraman who will decide about the appropriate lens, lighting and the camera movements.

The shooting:

When everybody on the set is ready for shooting director comes forward for the take. Before the take is announced last minute puffing and touch up by makeup artiste is taken up on actors, hair dresser moves in with his comb and mirror, costume assistant moves in to remove wrinkles on their costumes. Sometimes it is irritating before the shot as it disturbs the mood but it is an important activity before the take that should be allowed to be completed soon and peacefully. Other instructions should be passed on early. The process of a 'take' can be performed systematically with the following steps:

1.First of all an assistant director calls for '**silence**' to attract attention of everybody to be quiet and create silence before the take. This call means that unit is ready for a take. The watchman on the entry points on the location and the studio gate are also made aware about the take with the sounding of alarm bell . Outside the studio a *'Red light'* is switched on to inform people outside to know and prohibit any body to enter in during the take.

2.The director then asks if everybody is '**ready'.**

3.The assistant orders '**start sound'** to begin recording. The sound recordist then switches on his recorder to record the sound and waits for the recorder to attain its '**standard speed'.** The recordist then informs the cameraman '**started'** or '**recording on'**. This indication may be given by the recordist either by words, green light signal or physical indication.

4.After recording is started the assistant cameraman informs others saying **'camera rolling'** . once the camera is on, the assistant cameraman checks the camera speed by a *'Techometer'.* The moment speed is normal he calls for the clapper boy to give **clap.** Here it may be remembered that film camera runs at the standard speed of 24 frames/second while a digital camera on 25 frames/ second.

5.**Clapper boy** announces the details of the scene like scene no., shot no. and take no. while facing the *wooden clap board* in front of the camera. After the announcement he closes the clap that makes a **'clap sound'** which is recorded in the recorder and its closing visual is exposed in the camera. After this the clapper boy leaves the frame. This clap sound and picture helps editor to synchronize the picture and the sound of the take during the editing stage. Therefore the clap board exposure is very important in the take.

ANUKOOL PRODUCTIONS RASHMIN		
Scene No.	Shot No.	Take No.
45	12	1

18. Clap Board

When everything settles down after the clap, director orders the **'action'** and actors start performing their action and the dialogue followed by the camera movements.

During the process of taking if anything goes wrong the director has the authority to cut the shot in the middle. If there is something wrong from the point of view of the cameraman, he should still continue the shots till director says 'cut' as it is possible that minor mistake may be rectified by the editor later by using 'close up' or 'cut away' shots. Such shots can also be repeated for a flash back or a partial reconstruction of the scenes. Till there is no major mistake or the actor or director want to redo it, a 'retake' may be avoided to save money and time. Sometimes for a complicated shot or to save an actor from embarrassment the director may order a retake for safety purpose when he knows that the actor will do better in next take.

Few directors tell the cameraman that camera is here, it is this lens, here it will zoom, actor will move from this place to that place and so on to prove that they know everything but this attitude deprives actors and others' operational freedom and their creative contribution. Cameraman may have certain suggestion for the use of lenses and movements and actors may not be comfortable with the taking of the director therefore all these factors may be decided in consultation with everyone and shun his dictatorial attitude. He may accept a take as suggested by them for their pleasure. If he is not satisfied with technician's take , he may go for another take as he planned.

As a technical man I never preferred to personally involve in the technical departments when I am directing a film after I apprise them of my concept and vision. Thereafter I leave them to explore their best creative and imaginative skills. This makes them more responsible about their job. They get full functional freedom to take their decisions. If I am not happy with what I see through the view finder, I try to convince them and change their mind. I also prefer to have a technical rehearsal before the take to ensure if my vision is translated or not.

In some unusual situations when a director may not be by the side of the cameraman while shooting in aircraft or a helicopter or in some action sequences where multiple cameras are in use, director after discussing his requirements, should let him be on his own reposing his trust on him that he will do his best. some time director may believe that cameraman may not bring the shots needed by him then the he may ask him to get some '**additional shots**' with specific and unambiguous instructions.

The shots belonging to a common location or set, lighting arrangements and movements may be clubbed and taken one after the other deviating from the chronological order. This saves ample time and money that is wasted in shifting the camera, change in lighting etc. This also helps in winding up the scene early in the same location. This avoids repeat shifting from location or re-erecting a set, obtaining various permissions, boarding and lodging arrangements, location and equipment hiring. These factors may be considered while preparing a shooting plan.

XXXXX

'*A film editor is just not a cutter and joiner but he is the most creative person in the film crew who holds the keys of a 'good film'*.

Scene 10:

Film Editing:

'If you want to become a good director be a good editor first,' thus said the veteran film editor and director of Indian cinema **Hrishikesh Mukharjee.** What he meant is that the editor may be editing and shaping a film after the shooting but editing in real sense starts from the moment one decides to work on a screenplay. The editor may be implementing the principles of editing and maintain continuity of actions on the cutting table but the director and the cameramen are equally if not more responsible to execute them during the shooting. If they don't understand the principles of editing and rules of continuity, they will not be able to execute them in a shot, subsequently making the task of an editor much more difficult and sometimes impossible. There an editor cannot be blamed for flawed editing and entire responsibility for the flaws lies on the shoulders of a cameraman and the director so it is very imperative for them to understand and follow the basic elements of editing during and after the shooting.

'What is film Editing?' no other definition has generated as many interpretations as that of Film Editing. Everyone takes the liberty to interpret it with his narrow understanding, some call it 'Rejecting unwanted shots and put them in order of the story' while some call it 'Acceptability of film shots'. Some people relate it to the more popular concept of Editing of news papers and periodicals which 'compiles the written materials received from different sources and dump the rest which does not find a place in the news print'.

These interpretations reflect general ignorance about the concept and purpose of Editing whether it is for print material or the film material. My purpose here is not to devote more space for discussions on the differences and comparisons in editing procedures for print media and visual media which includes primarily film and television but to guide the students and professionals of cinema who restrict 'Film Editing' to its mere technical procedures and within the space of an Editing room. The editing is beyond the limited scope as perceived by people in general and film professionals in particular.

A *film editor* is just not a cutter and joiner but he is the most creative person in the film crew who holds the keys of a 'good film'. A well shot film can be ruined by an unimaginative editor and a "poorly shot" film can be made interesting by the editor's vision. The job of an editor can best be compared with that of a chef who with the best ingredients at his disposal prepares delicious and lip licking delicacies by utilizing his innovative skills combined with proper quantity of ingredients and timing of heating or cooling the stuff while other may spoil the taste by his lack of knowledge, innovation and dedication.

Editing of a film cannot be confined with the role and responsibilities of an editor but it begins at the moment a writer picks up his pen to scribble the idea of a film and it extends to the director, cameramen, sound recordist and sound editor to other technicians in the crew. No serious efforts have been made in the past to define the exact scope of editing for other technicians therefore the entire process of editing has been confined to the editor's table which is aesthetically not correct. Delinking the process of editing from other technicians including the director is not only an injustice to the poor guy called the 'Film Editor' but also wrongly absolves them to share their legitimate responsibility putting an unnecessary burden and onus of making a good film only on the Editor.

This is important to know that a poorly shot film by an inefficient technical crew can hardly make a good film on editing table with qualitatively poor ingredients even if an editor splits his hair and breaks his head on the walls so it is always not proper to blame an editor for 'bad editing' or a 'bad film' therefore it can be rightly surmised that '*if a film is good, everybody involved is responsible and if a film is bad , it is only the director who is responsible for the fiasco*' and he should be ready to share the blame for the reasons that 'A director is considered to be the *captain of the ship* and it is his responsibility to sail or sink the ship.

With the above arguments, it will not be appropriate to limit the process of film editing to the confines of four walls of the editing room. *Mechanical Editing* of a film is not the beginning of a creative process but its culmination. Broadly film editing can be defined as' *An arrangement of shots as per the chronological order and timing envisaged in a story or screen play,*' but it can be at best be said to be a physical process only that began with silent cinema when the film editing was limited to physically cutting and joining the shots of various activities and events in chronological order for a continuous projection.

While the principles of editing are devised to be followed by editor they have to be executed by the director and the cameraman during the shoots. If they fail to follow the rules of *'continuity'*, editor will not be able to rectify them on editing table.' Therefore following rules of continuity are as important for an editor as they are for the director, cameraman and the actors.

Editing:

When the shooting is completed, the exposed film negative is sent to film laboratory for develop and print. The sound recorded on a ¼" tape is transferred on the relevant gauge of optical film or magnetic tape. At this time recordist must ensure that sound is transferred in the standard speed of 24 frame/second otherwise it will not synchronize. The first unedited print is called' **Rush Print'** or '**work print'** which is used by the editor for editing purposes.

Once the editor receives the rush print and corresponding sounds, he then sorts them out according to the scenes and keeps them in separate boxes with the details of the scene on the top.. Thereafter he synchronizes the picture and sound by matching the clap with its corresponding sound exposed before the 'action', on the *synchrometer*. This process is continued till all the shots are synchronized and assembled as per the script. As is a normal practice this assembled material is jointly seen by the director, cameraman, editor, and the producer where they share their ideas about the concept and give suggestions to the editor accordingly. The editor marks the **'best take** ' in case of multiple OKs of the same shot in consultation with the director and the cameraman thereafter he starts cutting the film according to scenes and actor's performance, Speed and rhythm, camera placement and angles, dimension of the images etc. while making a rough cut director and the editor have the flexibility to make changes in the order of the shots and the scenes , some special visual effects may be created which otherwise are possible during the shoots. Now such effects are created in the computer graphics in digital format.

Continuity

The pre-requisite for an uninterrupted flow of a visual action and emotional expression when projected through the series of scenes is its **'Visual continuity'**. A moving action of the scenes after divided in shots is captured in the form of still photographs of celluloid frames. When these frames are projected through a film projector in the prescribed international standard running speed of 24 frames/second or 25 frames/second for digital projection, these still photographs come alive. These frames run one after another in the prescribed speed to complement its previous and preceding movement to take the action forward from one frame to the next. It means that every action in the frames has a direct relation with its previous and the subsequent movement. If it is not so then the scene lacks the continuity of the idea as envisaged in the scene and the flow in physical action. It may be remembered that a screenplay consists of many scenes and a scene consists of many 'shots' so a *shot* is the primary unit of a scene, that's why we discuss the *'shots'* and not the *'frames'* with reference to a scene. But if a frame is meaningless and irrelevant the shot too will be meaningless and irrelevant thus making a scene ineffective as a scene is the end result of the juxtaposition of many shots. It is the reason why a cameraman and the director concentrate more on the composition of a frame as whatever is seen in the frame forms the visual content of a scene therefore the director and the cameraman should be very careful and attentive to maintain continuity while composing and designing a frame.

When screenplay is in the process of being written it should be ensured that every scene has a definite meaning and the dimension,it should be expressed by the juxtaposition of shots. A slight deviation from it may spoil the entire scene. In the suspense or mystery films, directors have some freedom to deviate while taking few shots not confirming to defined continuity but it should be relevant to create drama or deepen the mystery.

Screen Direction:

When we talk of *screen direction* it is about the movement of the characters on the screen from one direction to another. It is very important to maintain continuity of movement. Normally a character on screen moves from left to right or right to left, Forward movement 'towards the spectators' or 'moving away with his back (Trail away)' from the audience. Before taking a decision on the screen direction the purpose of the movement and destination of the characters must be clearly defined.

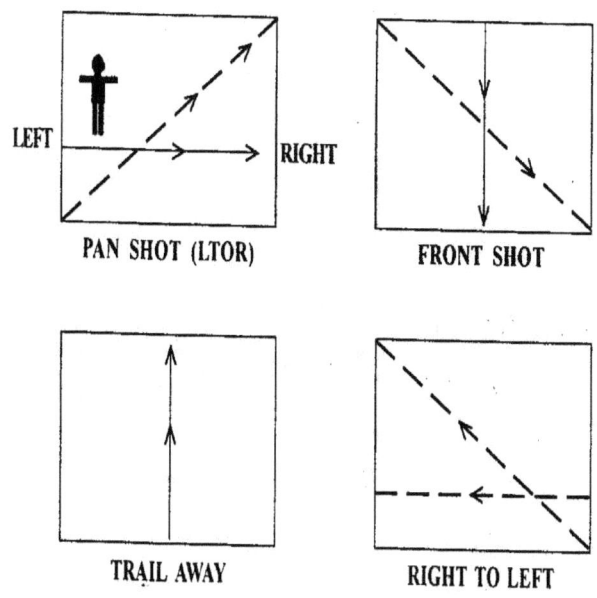

PAN SHOT (LTOR)   FRONT SHOT

TRAIL AWAY   RIGHT TO LEFT

19a..Screen Direction

If character A walks from left to right that means the character has to reach a subject or an object placed in the right . This movement also informs people that the destination of character A is on the right direction. If he changes his direction in the next shot that means he is going away from his destination, character or an object therefore this sudden change in the screen direction will be misconceived. If character A has to change his direction for a purpose then the purpose and his destination has be established prior to his about turn to avoid confusion about his motive.

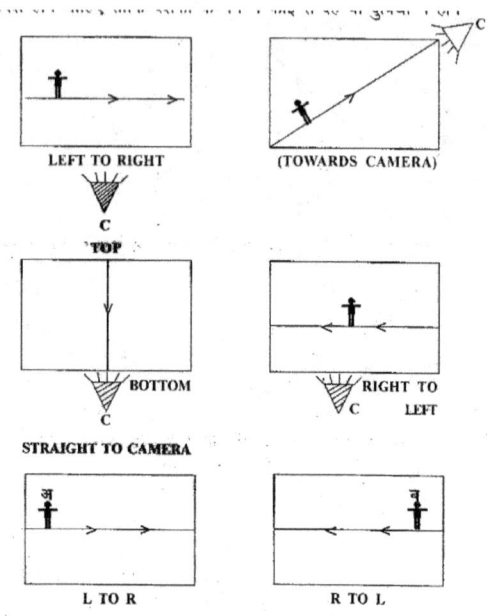

19b. Screen Direction

If in two different shots of the same scene, two persons move in the same direction, it does not mean that they would be meeting at a point. If director wants them to meet at some point, he has to show them moving in opposite directions . The movement of A walking from left to right while B walks from right to left is an indication that they are going to meet soon at a point. This technique is very commonly used to show conflicting situations, mystery and confrontation between two or more people or groups provided they approach each other from different directions. Such movements add interest and drama to the scene.

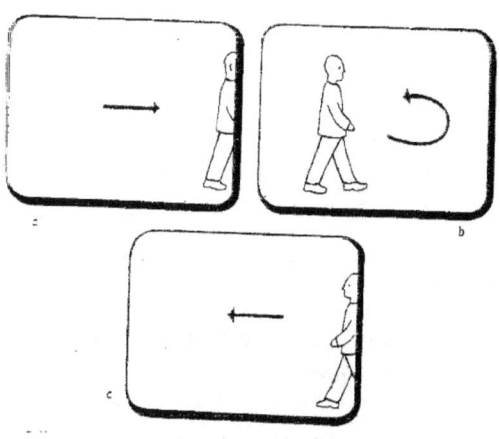

19c. Change in direction

If all the characters move in the similar direction it would be monotonous and boring therefore director while using different angles and distances also applies different direction of the movements of the characters and the objects however if required direction can always be changed with an indication of the same. The easiest way to show it is by the character choosing to take a turn to other direction to make the audience aware about the change in his movement and the further direction. This will not only maintain continuity of his movements but also avoid a continuity distraction that would be created by sudden cut to another direction.

Neutral shots:

Some shots are neutral n character as they have no direct bearing on the scene such as crowd, market, traffic, trees and forest, clouds, sunrise and sunset and other objects. They are used as 'inter cut' or to give a small pause or to change a camera angle and position. The moving objects like horse race, aircraft flying and train etc too can be used for the purpose. These shots have no distinct sense of direction and are used to change the screen direction. *Neutral shots* are one of the best transition devices to break the monotony of the scene. After their use director can change anything such as a location, time or the characters.

Reverse angle:

The shots   with two or more characters in the frame do not pose any continuity problems in Reverse angles.

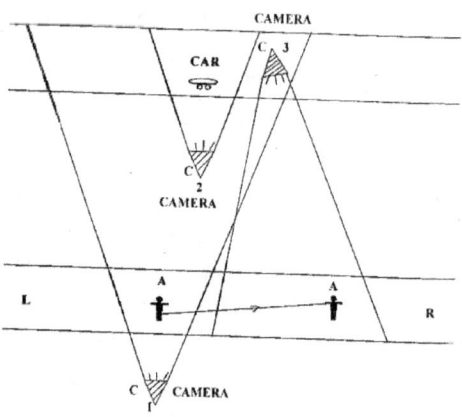

20. Reverse angle

In shot 1 character A is seen moving from left to right. After shot 2 of a car, shot 3 is taken in reverse angle in which character A is seen moving from right to left from the view point of the camera. The shot 2 of the car which is a neutral shot when juxtaposed between shot 1 and 3, the continuity jerk has been neutralized. So with the use of an insert, cut away or a neutral shot the director can alter his camera position or angle to reverse position or angle. Similarly if a character is moving in neutral direction i.e. coming to the camera or moving away from the camera, the next shot can be a reverse angle or position shot.

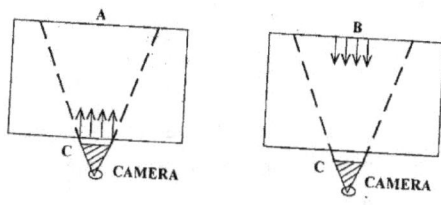

21. Neutral angle

Imaginary Line:

Imaginary Line or *Central-line Line* is decided from the movement of the character and not from the placement of the camera. Since this line is not visible it is called' **Imaginary Line or central-line Line'.** This line is considered to decide the screen direction and the camera placement. By managing this line the direction of the movement of characters and the objects is defined. If character A moves from left to right, it means that camera is placed to the right of the person. when camera is placed in the right side , the character will always be seen moving L-R therefore the director should decide camera position according to the movement of the character and maintain continuity of screen direction. If this simple principle of continuity is understood there will be no distraction in the continuity of screen direction. In case the character's movement is long and to the different direction, this rule may be cautiously applied as there is a possibility of confusion about camera positions.

The same rule may also be applied when many people are talking in the same position by considering sitting position of each person and the direction of his looks. In such shots an establishment shot is essential to establish every ones' position. The imaginary line is defined with the placement of the characters and their direction of looks. Camera should be positioned after careful consideration of the same.

Eye line continuity:

When there are two or more number of people, group or a crowd, maintaining *'Eye line continuity'* during the shoot is essential. **Eye line continuity** means the level of vision from the perspective of the viewers. The simple method of application of this rule is taking a long shot from the top angle in the beginning to establish the place and the atmosphere whether it is a Party scene or a congregation, agitation or a committee meeting, a marriage or a procession, a top angle in long shot clearly indicates the purpose of the shot. This shot is also called **'Master shot'.** Many of such Master shots may be taken in between the process of action which can be cut in between the scene to remind audience about the occasion and the ambience. It is because when camera concentrates on two or three persons, audience's attention is centered on those few people only and they ought to forget about other parallel happenings in the scene.

While a Long shot is taken to establish the position of the people or the group, any other action or movement by other characters should be taken in separate shots to keep the audience informed about this activity ,for example in a marriage or a Party sequence different type of additional shots may be taken to dramatize the scene, to maintain continuity, to show ambience, to establish other characters, their habits etc. These additional shots are very helpful to be used as an insert, cutaways, or intercut.

Moving shots in reverse angle:

A shot taken in different angles from a moving object like a train, a car or a cart may create lot of confusion in the direction of movement. It means, in one shot the background will be moving from left to right while in other it may be from right to left while the position of the persons sitting will remain unchanged. This may create a directional confusion in the mind of viewers. They will sometime see an object moving in one direction while in other it will be moving in reverse direction. This creates a distraction in the flow and a continuity jerk is noticed. The mistake is very common even with the most experienced directors therefore director should avoid taking shots in various direction and shoot only in the direction of movement. This does not mean that director is prohibited to undertake this misadventure. He can do so by applying the rule of 'Imaginary line' carefully. In fact management of Imaginary line is basically a cameraman's responsibility.

22.

Reverse

Move.

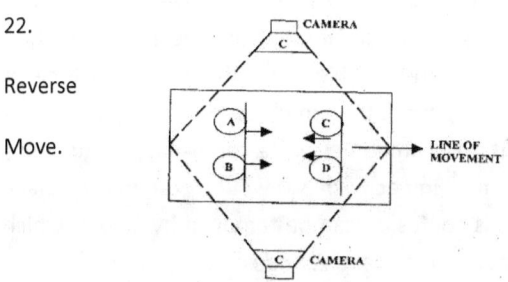

Screen time Management:

The real time or total time span of a story, happening is very long which could be in days, months or years while the entire story has to be condensed and told within the restricted time of two hours or so. Normal screening time of an Indian film is about 160 minutes but most of the films produced in English and other foreign languages range between 100 minutes to 200 minutes. All the stories including historical or mythological sagas have to be narrated with in this limited time without compromising with the emotional impact and illusion of time, therefore the real time of an event or a scene is condensed. This time is called *'Screen Time'*. The process of condensing real time or *'time condensation'* by the writer and the director during writing of screen play is crucial. In this process the screen time from the audience's view point should be natural and smooth. They should have an illusion of real time when they experience an event happening on the screen.

There are many devices to manage screen time such as fades, dissolves, wipes, montage etc which can be created optically in the film laboratory or by digital special effects creator in the computer.

1.Fades: If a film is divided in many scenes every scene is like a chapter of a book. Every scene contains special information about an event, emotions, objectives, the place and time of action in a specific period. If all these scene are juxtaposed by a 'direct cut' , it may sometime create confusion and audience may lose some impact they would otherwise have experienced. This confusion can be removed by *'Fades'* which are of two types-1. *Fade in* and 2. *Fade out*.

A. **Fade in-** It is used in the beginning of the scene when the image gradually appears from the dark.

B. **Fade out-** This is used in the end of the scene. In fade out the ongoing visual is gradually lost in the dark.

Fades are very common *'transitional device'* that have been used since the beginning of cinema to migrate from one scene to another and to establish 'time lapse ', 'change of a location or setting'. They indicate the change of a scene when fade out and fade in occurs in the same place one after another.

2.Dissolve: The process of simultaneous fade in and fade out of preceding and subsequent visuals is a 'dissolve' that defines passage of time or change of place. Dissolves are an expression of variety of ideas or a thought process. Normally with a series of dissolves a special massage is conveyed therefore dissolves have to be preplanned for a specific purpose and communication of a thought or series of ideas to achieve desired effect.

3.Montage: Juxtaposition of number of unrelated shots or actions to convey another cumulative meaning is a montage which is generally used in short, educational and fiction films to communicate a specific idea, thought or information. Montage can be interestingly created by direct cuts or dissolves. It injects excitement in the mood that takes the audience to a particular period, place or emotions. Montage is a very common device in cinematic expressions.

With the cinema taken over entirely by digital technology the film editing too transformed itself to digital process where use of celluloid material is reduced to minimum except for making final prints. The entire material shot on celluloid is transferred to digital data and preserved in *'Hard discs'*. Thereafter the film is edited on computers. While the basic principles of editing remain the same, operational process has undergone through tremendous changes. Digital process of editing too has reduced the total time frame of post shooting activities to a great extent thus saving lot of money, human energy and interventions in handling celluloid pieces of films and space to keep hundreds of film tins in the cranky space of an editing room.

Dubbing and Re-recording:

The dialogues in a fiction film constitute about 75% of total sounds used in a film. These dialogues are first recorded on location along with the take of the shots. Rest of the sound which includes sound effects, back ground music, songs and other special sound effects are recorded later in the post shooting phase. While the editor is busy editing the film with the pilot track of the dialogues the recordist simultaneously prepares for *'Dubbing'* and other sounds required for the film. It may be noted that songs are recorded prior to shoots and played back for the actors to perform in front of the camera. The Back ground music is recorded after the rough cut of the film is ready. Once the rough cut is over music and sound departments swing in to action. Recordist starts dubbing the film to replace the pilot track that carries lot of noise and unwanted sound of the location. After dubbing this pilot track is discarded.

During the dubbing, the actor looks at the scene projected on the screen with pilot track heard by him through head phones.

Here the pilot track guides him to speak the same words what he had spoken during the shoot. The actor speaks the dialogues again synchronizing his words with the lip movement of the character on screen. Here again the standard speed of recording and the projection is maintained by interlocking the machines.. It is reminded that the standard speed in digital recording is 25 frames/second unlike 24 frames/second of the celluloid form. Thus in the dubbing process all the noise and unwanted location sounds are eliminated and a 'clear dialogue track' is obtained.

Other than the dialogues there are many external and inherent sound effects that emanate from the ambience. The specific actions of the performers like footsteps create incidental sounds while the sound of rains and thunder are general effects or natural sounds that are required to create mood and atmosphere. Most of the natural effects are available in sound libraries, if not they are to be recorded or artificially created along with incidental effects in the studio. Once this is done editor synchronizes them with the scenes in separate sound tracks. Similarly Back ground music suitable to the mood and requirement of the scene is recorded and matched with the visuals in separate tracks. Song and dance performances are kept in other separate tracks and not mixed with the back ground music. There can be more than one track for particular type of sound such as dialogues, back ground music, sound effects and songs etc. Thus at the end of all the sounds synchronized and marked with the film, there are multiple number of tracks on the table to be mixed. The editor prepares a 'dope sheet' to guide the recordist about the markings and the timing of the sound to appear in the film.

Mixing or the rerecording is carried in specially designed recording studios where there is a facility to run multiple track simultaneously In this process the recordist re- records the music, effects , dialogues, song and dance tracks separately for the convenience. It is followed by final mixing of sound tracks which does not include dialogue tracks. The exclusive final mixed sound track is called 'International track' which is used later for dubbing the film in various local and foreign languages. Once international track is ready the dialogue track is finally taken up for mixing and the film is ready as it will look in the theatre.

After Re-recording is completed the picture track and the sound tracks are then transferred to optical sound and picture negative for making the print of the film in the laboratory . There are similar '**key numbers'** printed on one side of the negative and the positive stock. These numbers are very useful and required to be matched at the time of Negative cutting'. It is done on a synchrometer by keeping picture negative and work print parallel by the negative cutters.

 The first print is called '**Answer Print'** as the same is used to detect any defects in the sound and the picture quality, color corrections and for the censor purposes. Normally this answer print is not released in theatre but some producers send it to remote places where quality of the print is no body's concern thus saving the cost of making one print. This print is also called 'Married print' due to the togetherness of picture and sound on the same stripe..

Sometimes adhering to audience's reactions producer and the director decide to reedit part of the film to increase its acceptability by adding or deleting certain scenes or songs which were not used earlier due to limited length. It is also possible that few scenes are revised in the script and shot again to be incorporated in the film. In this process entire post shooting process is repeated for the specific reels. While such modifications in the film don't ensure film's success producer , the directors do not take chance to ignore it.

XXXXXX

'In every civilized society and the nation this aspect of cinema has been carefully weighed to find out *'what and how much'* an average viewer should be allowed to watch on a film screen to keep them with in checks of social and moral limits'.

11:
Film censorship or certification

It is believed that a moving picture is thousand times more effective than a still photograph. The moving pictures though may not be capable to change a society but they have the potential to create a strong opinion as they make deep impression in the minds of people. It has been proved time and again that many criminals are inspired by films for their crime therefore there is always a need to restrict the depiction of and comments on certain issues and things that may smash social and cultural traditions of a society. The identification of audience with the characters on screen is so strong that they follow their footsteps and emulate their actions which they find palatable. Impact of films on an impressionable mind should be judged from the perception of an average viewer and not from the view point of those who have a developed intellectual level and can reason beyond visual images on screen.

Censorship:

The word 'censorship' has been coined by those ruling establishments who wanted to restrict anti establishment ire to keep their country under their control and united under any circumstances. The censorship is practiced more by rulers having dictatorial tendencies and are intolerant for any criticism against them. The things started changing where democracy began to thrive and established its hold in the governance in many countries however censorship is still stringent in monolithic societies.

In every civilized society and the nation this aspect of cinema has been carefully weighed to find out 'what and how much' an average viewer should be allowed to watch on a film screen to keep them with in checks of social and moral limits. These limits have different parameters in different societies due to their accepted value system therefore every nation has established its own mechanism to put these checks and balances in order which is applied on media including cinema.

The mechanism of these restrictions varies from **'censorship'** to **'certification'** of cinematic material. In film censorship there is an order to 'delete or not to show anything not permitted or objectionable'. In this system producer normally has no say in the matter. They have no other option than just to comply with the order of authorities. Non compliance of such orders is considered a punishable crime. In the certification methods, generally no force is used for compliance as the certificates are issued in such a way that the content of a film is suitable to a particular 'age group'. If a producer wants to obtain a certificate for any other age group he has to mend his content accordingly. Therefore a certification system which is used in many western countries is considered more democratic and acceptable than the censorship.

India is leading in the field of film production. It is one of the top film producing countries with more than a thousand fiction films produced annually. Beside this there is significant number of documentary, shorts and animation and advertizing films made each year. There is a chain of more than 13000 cinema screens including single screen and the multiplexes, video parlors and cable television that screen Indian fictions and employ millions of people from film actors to lowly paid film technician. With such wide spread business opportunities available to producers their efforts to apply every trick of the trade to earn huge profits cannot be denied however this profit does not come to a producer without its pitfalls and neck to neck completion and pulling the carpet from below the feet. They face competition and challenges from television industry that had spread its wings far and wide, video piracy that has spread its tentacles beyond the geographical limits, cable and satellite that provide entertainment in the comforts of a drawing room at much economical cost. In this climate of cut throat competition the producer is ready to compromise with his social and cultural limits and his individual dignity to any extent. The Indian cine goers consist of a big chunk of those young and adolescent children and those who are deprived of their basic needs for whom entertainment is a myth. Producers target this disgruntled section of society and provoke their basic instincts which are suppressed in Indian social, cultural and national milieu. Unfortunately Indian people were given freedom without preparing them for it. The situation is not much different in many other developing countries as well. There comes the need to put a check on such frivolous actions of so called entertainers and set some dignified restrictions on their freedom of expressions.

Many developed nations have established a fool proof system to overcome the issue of cinema exhibition. They set up an authority precisely for this purpose and handover a certificate for exhibition of films after due deliberations and revisions in the visual and audio material submitted to it by the producer. This certificate is still commonly called **'censor certificate'** which is essential for a producer to obtain before he exhibits his film anywhere in the country and abroad. This 'certificate' is not the end of the issues which are frequently violated by the people in film trade at various levels. Though there is a legal framework available to deal with such misadventures , it is difficult to execute the laws of violations from the state to the district levels due to multiplicity of law enforcement agencies.. There are many NGOs and voluntary organizations who come forward to inform the authorities of such violations but it is more said than done. Censorship violations are not considered to be the most serious ones so less attention is paid for these crimes. General public is largely unconcerned about them .The television and satellite revolution along with cyber technologies have made film certification more vulnerable against any onslaught.

Where censorship is still continued, the censor board is demonized by those who plead against any attack on the **'freedom of expression'** of film makers Some do it to score some brawny points for creative reasons and few do it for political mileage. Everybody has his reasons to support and oppose the existence of film censor board. Many of them oppose it purely for commercial reasons to get free pre-release publicity and create controversy to attract audience to the ticket window by simply highlighting routine cuts advised by the censor committees. Censor committees advise producer to revise their content by deleting, adding or improving certain portions of the content which according to them may not be appropriate for general public that mainly include vulnerable section of the society with an average intelligence quotient, adolescent and children or those who may feel that their religious sentiments or modesty is hurt.

Freedom of expression:

The media , press or television News are more or less independent in their functioning though there may be some difference of opinion about it but is the media really free even without interference of the ruling dispensation? Most of the print and News television establishments are guided by the political policies of their owners so it is very difficult to say that media is absolutely free . This debate of freedom of expression is more a personal choice of those who forget that there is no absolute freedom of expression anywhere in the world. If this would have been so, why film censorship or media regulators existed everywhere in one form or the other? Though there is significant amount of freedom of expression, there is always a **red line** which one cannot and should not cross for many reasons. The democracies around the world encourage them to practice little constraints and not cross the red line that hurts social and national interests . Censorship and regulators are an answer to the proponents of anti censorship campaign. In fact the job of a regulator is not to muzzle independent freedom of expression but to warn them about the red line they must respect.

The constitutions of many democratic nations provide complete freedom of expression but it should not be read as unlimited or absolute freedom. There are certain restrictions in expressions in the interest of sovereignty, in the defense of national freedom, security of the state, friendly relations with the neighboring countries or foreign state, social order and discipline, morality, contempt of court, defamation , the offences and crimes that incite violence and anarchy etc. In cinematic expressions censor board has to search for a fine balance between freedom of creative expression and the social and national interest. Since these regulations are in the interest of the society at large it is the sovereign duty of everybody to adhere to them.

XXXXX

12:
Glossary

Accelerated Motion: The natural speed of an action in the shot is fastened. It is opposite to 'slow motion'.

Actual Sound: This is the sound which occurs from the actual actions in the scene as actors delivering dialogues, telephone bell, footsteps etc.

Back Projection: When shooting in a studio there is a moving background behind the actors which is projected from a projector kept behind a screen.

Bloop; The triangular shaped Bloop is pasted on the joints to stop unnecessary and irritating 'thud' sound coming from the joints of negative or positive film material.

Bridging Shots: when a continuity jerk is observed between the joints and juxtaposition of two shots, Bridging shots are joined in between the two.

Close Shots: a shot is taken by a camera kept near to the subject or object. Zoom lens is also used to take close shots or medium shots when a subject or object is at a distance.

Camera Angle: an angle to place a camera by which a visual is proposed to be seen.

Cheat Shots: Splitting shots of a dangerous act from a miraculous distance or danger to give a feeling of complete action.

Clap board: A wooden clap board used before a take to give details of the scene, shots and number of takes and clap to synchronize the visual and sound in editing.

Clapper Boy: The person who speaks the details of the scene written on the board and claps before the take.

Close Medium Shot: The shot between close and medium distance generally from knee to head.

Close up: very close to the subject or object to show the details. Generally it is only the face of a person.

Commentary: Explanation or comments running parallel to the visuals.

Commentative sound: The sounds like Back ground music, general atmospheric sounds etc. which are not produced by an action but are felt psychologically along with the scene. Opposite to 'Actual sounds'.

Continuity sheet: A prescribed format which has various columns to be filled with the details of scenes/shots.

Continuity man: The technician who writes about the details of a scene /shot in a prescribed form.

Continuity Title: The caption to link two disconnected scenes for continuity.

Crane shot: Specially designed crane for shooting purposes where a camera is placed to take a shot.

Cross cutting: showing of parallel actions taking place in different locations at the same time to enable the viewers to see both the actions simultaneously one after another without missing the other.

Cutter: The technician who does the physical part of editing.

Cutting Print: The positive print which is used for editing the film. This print is also called the 'Rush print' or 'Rushes'.

Dissolve: Emergence of a shot from the dark with parallel fade out of another one with in the same duration and length gradually. It is decided by parallel markings of fade in and fade out on both the shots on a synchrometer.

Dubbing: It is re recording of dialogues originally recorded on location during shooting. The actors reproduce their dialogues in the basic or any other language in a recording studio.

Dupe Negative: The Duplicate negative which is different from the original negative is made from inter- positive print. This is used to make multiple prints of the film for release purpose.

Duplicate Print: The print made out of the dupe negative.

Establishing shot: It is generally a Long shot used in the beginning to establish the location of the scene.

Effect track: A separate sound track for sound effects in addition to dialogue and music tracks.

Extra shot: The additional shots taken during the shoot.

Fade in: The shot emerge slowly from the dark to full illumination.

Fade out; The fully visible or illuminated shot gradually vanishes in to dark.

Flash back: the scene that takes the viewers to the past. It is used to show a past event or experiences.

Footage: the length of film stripe or a scene measured in feet.

Frame: one of the transparent (Transparency) pictures in the series on the celluloid stripe.

Full shot: Full visual of a subject or object seen in the frame. From head to toe.

Joint: A joint of two celluloid pieces.

Jump: Breaking of the continuity of time and action to proceed to another time and action.

Leader: An ordinary film stripe added before the first frame of the film (Positive or Negative) to thread in the projector/ printing machine. Generally it is a negative film exposed in the sun. There are special leaders for the final film prints and the negatives.

Library shot: the film material not shot for the purpose of a film and preserved separately in the archive or a film library.

Long shot: it is like full shot from head to toe with some additional head space. Long shots also denote wider visual perspective. It is generally used to establish a location or a place.

Married Print: A film print combined with visuals and sound in the same stripe.

Mask: Hiding a portion of a visual seen from the camera. It is done in the camera itself.

Master shot: A shot containing the entire scene in a single shot to guide the editor about the scene. Some directors take master shots for creative purposes.

Medium Shot: Closer than the long shot but away from the range of close shots.

Mixer: An equipment to mix separate sound tracks at the time of rerecording.

Montage: Juxtapositions of disconnected shots to construct a scene with a new meaning.

Multiple exposures: Exposing a frame more than once. It is done to create special visual effects.

Mute Negative: The sound negative which does not contain sound modulations or sound track. It is used to fill the gaps in the sound negative.

Mute print: It is also called 'Silent sound Track (SST) which is used to fill the gaps in the sound positive or 'cutting print' during the editing.

Narrator: A character who explains story or event in a fiction film or a commentator who explains about the scene in non-fiction films.

Optical: Visual effects like dissolve, fades and wipes, super impositions etc. created on a special machine in a film laboratory.

Optical printer: A special machine which creates a scene with the help of a lens and also to make reduction print, special or trick effects.

Over the shoulder: The Camera on the back of the shoulder of a character.

Pan: Moving the camera from left to right or right to left from a fixed position.

Pan Shot: A shot taken by moving camera left and right.

Parallel action: Showing different events occurring at the same time one after another.

Play back: Re play of a pre recorded music track at the time of shooting to synchronize the action with the sound. Play back is generally used for shooting songs and dance sequences.

Post synchronization: Matching of pre recorded sound effects and other sounds with the visuals after the shooting.

Print: Final copy of a film.

Relational Editing: Creating a relationship between the shots during the editing.

Re-recording: Mixing of multiple sound tracks.

Retake: Shooting a shot again.

Rewind, Rewinder: Winding the film rolls on a machine called 'rewinder'.

Rough cut: First assembly of selected shots to construct a scene.

Slow cutting: Keeping the shots lengthy or for more duration to slow down the pace of the scene. It is reverse of the 'fast cutting.'

Slow motion: Slower than actual speed of an action.

Sound track: on the sides of film stripe the sound modulations or track run parallel to the visuals.

Stock shot: shots preserved in an archive or a film library.

Super impose: Printing of two or more shots on the similar place and length of the film to see them one over another.

Synchronization, Synch: Matching the visuals and sounds parallel to each other so that visuals are seen and sound is heard simultaneously during the projection as if it is coming from the visuals.

Synchronizer: An equipment to synch visuals and sounds in parallel tracks. It can accommodate up to four or six tracks.

Synchronous sounds: The sounds which are synchronized with the visuals or can be synchronized to show the visuals as source of the sounds in the scene.

Take: Recording a shot in the camera.

Tilt: Moving the camera up and down from a fixed position.

Track, Tracking: Moving the camera straight forward or backward on a trolly or any other device. The word 'track' is also used for sound tracks.

Trolley (straight and round): A cart on wheels on which the cameraman sits to take the shot in whatever direction he wants to move.

Truck shot: Shot taken from a truck, trolley, car or any other vehicle.

Wild shooting: Shooting without sound where no sound is recorded with the action.

Wild sound: Recording without visuals. This sound is matched with the scene later.

Wipe: A device to show the transition of the scene like dissolve and fades.

XXXXX

Bibliography:

- **Kuldeep Sinha** is a Film graduate from Film and Television Institute of India, Pune with an experience of over 30 years.
- Written, Produced, Edited & directed more than 200 Short films on variety of subject.
- Author of Books on '**Film Direction'**, '**Screenplay writing' and** '**Film Editing'** and a coffee table Book on Legendry Play Back Singer of Indian Cinema **MOH. RAFI.**
- Author of anthologies **Kashish, Siskiyaan**. & **Dastak** of original short stories.
- Authored a Book on Personality Development **Galion se chaurahe tak.**
- Author of English novels-**The Darkness in the Arc, Neither , Behind the moving Images.**
- Editor- **Documentary Today** (A magazine on Non-fiction films)
- **Rashmin**: Marathi Translation of anthology: *'Kashish'*
- International Participation in Film festivals-Slovakia, Sweden, Berlin, Rome, Australia, India etc.

- **International Awards:**
  Non-conventional Energy Resources-Agro Film 84 Slovakia
  Non Conventional Energy Resources- Golden Ear Berlin.1984
  Non Conventional Energy Resources- International consumer film competition-Berlin1985
  Non Conventional Energy Resources- Boris Kidvic Award, International scientific film competition-Belgrade 1985.
  Services of tress-Silver Bunch, International film festival Santarem Portugal 1987
  Watershed Management- F.A.O. Award. slovakia1996
  Poultry Farming- F.A.O. Award, Slovakia 2005.

- **National film Awards:**
  Special Children-Special award 2005
  Hans Akela- Best Biographical film-2008
  Teejan Bai- Best Biographical Film 2002
  Vermiculture-Best Agriculture film 2000
  Tribal Women Artists- Best Art and culture film 2000
  From the land of Buddha to the land of Buddha-Best Historical Reconstruction film 2000
  In search of Excellence - Best Adventure and exploration film. 1998
  Tara Nath Shenoy-Best News Film 1986

- **Other Awards:**
  Police –your friend: Best documentary film, Maharashtra State Award 2002
  Anmol Patthar Bemole Zindagi: Best Documentary film-R.A.P.A. Award 2001

- **Special Honours:**
  - **Scroll of Honours:** for contribution in Indian cinema by Indian organization of mass communication and Institute of Broadcasting Mumbai.
  - **Life Time Achievement Award:** International centre for Cultural Relations, Mumbai.
  - **Hindi Sahitya Samman-** Ministry of Information & Broadcasting, Govt. Of India.
  - **Rajbhasha Shree-** Prasar Bharti (Govt. Of India) & Ashirwad Award Mumbai.
  - **Saraswat Samman-** Ashirwad Award, Mumbai.

- **Notable Films-**
  - **Rafi: We Remember you**
  - **Toote Pankh**
  - **Gandhi- an emerging reality**
  - **Through a lens starkly**
  - **No Room for fear.**
  - **Druzhba**
  - **India-Bhutan Friends forever.**

XXXXX